Satan's Looming Identity Crisis! The Final War in the Age of Reason

by

I. A. Mallone

DORRANCE PUBLISHING CO., INC.
PITTSBURGH, PENNSYLVANIA 15222

ISBN: 978-1-4349-0455-3
Printed in the United States of America

First Printing

For information or to order additional books, please write:
Dorrance Publishing Co., Inc.
701 Smithfield St.
Pittsburgh, Pennsylvania 15222
U.S.A.
1-800-788-7654
www.dorrancebookstore.com

Contents

Introduction

According to human beliefs ages ago, a predominant feature of Earth's identity was erroneously perceived to be that of a flat structure that seemed to be the floor of the universe. Another mistaken belief that still persists to this day is that the predominant feature of man's identity is one of a finite, sentient, material creature; one of an organic, personal, human being existing in an objective, physical universe. This book will show logically that not only one, but both of these concepts are erroneous beliefs. Both of these false beliefs have been resolved through intelligent reasoning that has understood and uncovered the respective principles underpinning them. In so doing, the faculty of intelligent reasoning has revealed the truth about both concepts. Although both of these mistaken identity concepts have been successfully resolved, most of us are aware of only one, the former, whose misconception inflicted the lesser negative impact upon man.

During man's struggle to gain a correct and useful understanding of the underlying principles of these or any subject or arena, one essential element is always necessary for success, the lack of which will always result in failures hindering further progress. That one, essential element is always intelligent reasoning. Seeking the correct understanding of an issue, intelligent reasoning cautiously moves forward, struggling from point to point, and is ever watchful to ensure the solid integrity and proof of every step taken. Intelligent reasoning battles against ignorance and mistaken beliefs by presenting arguments for its position. In these battles, not only is the outcome decided upon the integrity of the reasoning employed, but also upon the actual demonstrated proof of the position taken.

The struggle of intelligent reasoning versus erroneous beliefs and assumptions on these and other issues is not always an easy process. Take our modern technology as an example. In an excited or careless rush to succeed or progress, failures have arisen because it was falsely believed that the level of understanding underpinning an endeavor was sufficient; only later was it discovered to be woefully lacking. In cases like these, false beliefs and baseless assumptions were found to be supporting the reasoning process instead of the facts - misunderstanding and failure leads the way. Bridges collapse and rockets explode. We are then forced to go back over the ground of what was believed to be sound reasoning and find the culprit that has caused the failure. Failures do not yield automatically to success until this is painstakingly and exactly done. Erroneous beliefs or careless assumptions in the reasoning process do not produce correct understanding and success at all, but rather the contrary, as is always proven by their respective, demonstrated failures. Through a series of proofs of demonstrated successes and failures, progress is finally made when the erring beliefs and invalid assumptions are uncovered through a persistent application of sound, intelligent reasoning. In this process, a more mature understanding of the principle involved is revealed yielding greater and more consistent success, harmony, and progress.

Without these battles between fact and fancy, our modern world would never have developed. Technically, in the hands of ignorance and erroneous beliefs, even the common sense to seek shelter in a cave would have been denied to our caveman ancestors. Progress never occurs automatically. Behind every successful step taken forward, in any arena, lies the painstaking effort of intelligent reasoning that leads to correct understanding.

We have already been engaged in and measurably won many of these battles that have enriched our lives throughout history. Intelligent reasoning has fought and advanced our understanding in the arenas of agriculture, mathematics, physics, astronomy, chemistry, electricity, electromagnetism, thermodynamics, music, and biology, to name a few, that have all contributed to the wonderful technological and cultural achievements we take for granted and enjoy today.

Mastery of many subjects was not always an easy and straightforward process. The manner in which our present understanding of Earth and the solar system developed is a perfect example of intelligent reasoning struggling for acceptance against a cultural mindset of erring beliefs. As previously stated, at one time Earth was erroneously believed to be the flat floor of the universe. In this erring belief, the sun and other celestial bodies resided in and moved around the heavens above this "flat floor." Later, as intelligent reasoning forged ahead, these false beliefs were discarded and more accurate beliefs, although still not entirely correct, were accepted as the truth. By the third century B.C., Eratosthenes, a Greek mathematician, had determined that Earth was a sphere and calculated its rough circumference.[1] By the second century A.D., Ptolemy firmed up the concept that not only was Earth a sphere, but it was believed to be the center of the universe, commonly known as the geocentric model.[2] In these partially improved beliefs, Earth was correctly recognized to be a spherical planet, but the concept was still tainted with the erroneous belief that Earth was the center of the universe and the sun, stars, and other planets revolved around it. This geocentric model was believed to be true for quite some time, and it wasn't until 1543 that Copernicus shattered it by mathematically proving Earth revolved around the sun in what is known as the heliocentric model.[3] Although all individuals presenting new and improved ideas in any subject run into some resistance by opposing beliefs, Galileo's struggle for intelligent reasoning in the field of astronomy is one of the most famous examples. In his struggle, Galileo found considerable resistance from the Church in his support of the Copernican heliocentric model. In 1633 Galileo was actually put on trial by the Church for heresy.[4] This conflict illustrates a perfect example of baseless, erroneous beliefs at war with intelligent reasoning.

With the more correct understanding of the solar system, Earth still appeared flat to our limited human senses, but increased benefits and advantages for mankind were still realized, as they always will when a more accurate understanding of any subject is attained. Most notable was the development of celestial navigation, allowing mankind to expand trade routes, circumnavigate the globe, and eventually, when combined with the increased understanding of other sciences, exit the limitations of Earth and travel to the moon and beyond. All of these activities and accomplishments furthered our understanding of our surroundings and ourselves, compounding the benefits and advantages to mankind both collectively and individually, and we owe it all to the faculty of accurate, intelligent reasoning.

But just like these step-by-step developmental stages in earlier times, what if our present, modern concepts of the universe and the identity of man still contain mistaken beliefs that limit our present capabilities and, therefore, still need to be uncovered and corrected? Will we again cling to our commonly held beliefs defining our present "understanding" of man and the universe because we find them to be comforting and cherished possessions not to be upset or tampered with? As in the past, will we be unwilling to part with them and insist that the present modern concepts of the universe and the identity of man is the final word and are the "facts," closing the door on further revelations, benefits, and advantages? Or, will we be receptive and open minded to a new, more accurate understanding that once again challenges the present, "modern," "factual" concepts no matter how jarring and radical the new understanding may be? We know that, in time, we have always discarded false beliefs and concepts when intelligent reasoning has proven otherwise, and once again, intelligent reasoning with a more accurate and useful understanding is knocking on our door with new revelations in hand to benefit mankind collectively and individually. How long do we hold on to our cherished beliefs before we are willing to open the door this time? The march of intelligent reasoning never has been stopped, nor will it ever be stopped by contrary, erroneous beliefs, although the war of false beliefs versus reasoned facts continues to struggle on.

The subject of this book, *Satan's Looming Identity Crisis! The Final War in the Age of Reason* will examine this war of ideas where intelligent reasoning battles aggressive, mistaken beliefs point-by-point as to the true nature of the universe and the true identity of man. It answers the questions, Is the universe, life, and existence itself an actual physical reality within a time-space-matter framework containing seemingly finite birth-life-death cycles and other challenges and limitations for all things in it, or is it something else? Why did the universe happen? What is our purpose here? Why do some events seem so unfair and cruel, like disease, accidents, natural disasters, and wars? Why are we, as humans, locked in a cycle that begins with a birth, immediately commences to age, and has sickness and disease to contend with along with a limited life span that inevitably ends in death? Is the finite, material human being and its mind our true identity? Where are our minds located when we are living? In an organic brain that decomposes upon dying? Do our minds leave the brain and go on when we die, and if they do, where do they go? Do our minds leave the universe when we die? If they do, where to and how? Etc., etc. In this particular arena, where we sincerely seek to answer these questions, we are truly engaged in a final war, because in this arena truly lies the entirety or "all" of existence, containing the issues of the universe proper, life, death, and immortality. In this arena we finally uncover and conquer the aggressive cause of all discord, disease, limitation, and death and, in so doing, reveal our true identity.

But presently, in this war of ideas struggling to understand the true nature of the universe and our place in it, which side is winning and progressing? How much of our understanding of the universe and ourselves is still undermined with ignorance and false beliefs, and how much is based on sound intelligent reasoning of the facts? The answer to these questions and more will be battled out in the following pages as contending forces of intelligent reasoning and understanding take on the forces of aggressive and erroneous, baseless beliefs. In so doing, the goal is the same as in any other subject area: to intelligently reason and correctly understand the true nature of the facts and principles involved and thereby enjoy the increased benefits and advantages this understanding can provide.

For most of us, we never really questioned the validity of the physical universe containing seemingly finite birth-life-death cycles for everything in it, including ourselves, as anything but actual, hard, facts of reality or nature. In fact, to question the validity of the physical universe, along with the various material laws and things in it, would seem arrogant or almost blasphemous to some. Others may think it is simply beyond our ability to reason and understand the principles involved within such a seemingly enormous and intimidating proposition.

As in all other arenas where intelligent reasoning has been engaged in, it was noted that failure and lack of progress was always the proven result of erroneous beliefs and assumptions undermining the understanding. Success and rapid progress was always the proven result of correct understanding and was never the result of luck, gods smiling on our endeavors, or some other nonsensical, mysterious influence. In any subject where we desire to succeed, mistakes and failures are never tolerated. In fact, we always take great pride in our ability to root out the causes of failures, correct them, and thereby contribute to the success and enjoyment of the project at hand. Therefore, to be consistent in this age of accelerated advancements and bold technological conquests, we should also have the same courage, confidence, and most importantly, open minds in this theater as well, and engage ourselves in this final war of ideas to reason and work to correctly understand the true nature of the universe in which we seem to be such an integral part.

This final war, which must inevitably be fought out within the mind of each individual in order to understand his or her true identity and their place in the universe, is a series of battles between two contending forces. One force using weapons of aggressive, mistaken, erring beliefs and illusions versus the other, whose only weapon is a correct understanding of what is fact and what is not.[5] True, solid understanding can only be forged through intelligent reasoning. As will be shown, baseless beliefs are not only worthless, they are dangerous. But unfortunately, in this final arena where the subject and principle involved is your life and the universe you live in, you can't simply go to a store and buy the success and benefit of someone else's reasoning and understanding like, for example, purchasing a computer or some other high-tech item off the shelf that others have painstakingly reasoned to produce. Similarly, if one desires to become a successful mathematician, physicist, musician, etc., individuals with greater understanding in these respective subjects can only serve as guides to point the way; they can never perform another's own reasoning work for them. If you desire greater understanding and success, you must do the reasoning work yourself. No one else can do this work for you. Just like the subject of mathematics or physics as an example, a book and/or a teacher can guide or point the way but you alone must perform the reasoning work yourself. As in all other arenas, not only can individuals gain greater understanding and success through reasoning, but they may then go even further with their own reasoning and demonstrated proofs, thereby revealing even greater understanding for others to follow.

The intent of this book is not to entertain the masses but, it is hoped, to provide a substantial foothold for those sincerely seeking a greater understanding of their life and the universe they live in as revealed through the process of intelligent reasoning and its application. In obtaining a better understanding, they will lessen the occurrence of inharmonious failures due to mistaken beliefs, such as sickness, poverty, and discord, and reap the benefits and advantages due to intelligent reasoning—that of harmonious and continuous Life free from any discord, limitations, or even death. [6]

A famous actor once observed that he was so impressed with the intelligence and resultant achievements of mankind in his lifetime; he expected mankind to outwit death itself one day. This statement will be shown to be an accurate observation because death is, in fact, not an inevitable event in life but is really nothing more than a resultant failure that can be prevented. Thus, the cause of death can be understood, outwitted, and prevented. In fact, not only is death a failure that can be prevented, but sickness, disease, war, old age, crime, poverty, suicide, natural disasters, starvation, loneliness, greed, addictions, etc., are all failures that can be prevented as well. Unfortunately, and just as they do in all other arenas, failures will mindlessly continue until sound, intelligent reasoning is brought to bear on the false, erroneous beliefs and errors that are causing them. In all the past battles where we have struggled to untangle mistaken beliefs and errors, failures never once yielded to success as we sat down, did nothing, and hoped the problems would go away or just somehow change by themselves. Failures always just sat there and tenaciously held their ground until the cause of them was found through intelligent reasoning and the necessary corrections were made.

On the positive side, are not failures and limitations actually good experiences trying to instruct us and show us where there is an error in our beliefs of what is true and what isn't?[7] They seem to be whispering, "Take the clue. It has always been this way and always will be this way. We (failures and limitations) are not something in and of ourselves but are the result of mistakes and false beliefs and we simply won't go away until you understand what has caused us to appear, and you do have the reasoning faculty, intelligence, and ability to accomplish this. We can appear as mountains of granite, rock-solid, immovable, unchangeable failures, limitations, and woes, but when correct understanding is gained as to what caused these fearful and intimidating mountains to appear, they will disappear as soft wisps of summer air as they always do."

We are born, we tough it out, and for most people, we naturally hope, believe, and desire that after we die life continues on, it will somehow be automatically better, or we may fear it will be worse depending on our recent human behavior and beliefs. Still others may believe that death ushers in a complete cessation of life—like turning a switch off. In all cases our various beliefs reinforce the common view that death, eventually, seems normal and inevitable, and we just blindly accept it without any serious doubts challenging the validity of the process. We don't even view death as a failure that could have been avoided but accept it as a natural occurrence and then naturally hope for the best outcome based on our various dogmatic and mysterious beliefs.

If we erroneously believed $2 + 2 = 5$ to be true, while bridges fell down, rockets exploded, and checkbooks didn't balance, would we accept these failures along with the worldly-wise but submissive statement of "That is just the way it is," or would we find the cause of these failures, correct them, and enjoy the resultant success? In this book we will see that, when we are finally armed with a correct understanding of the true state of affairs, we can find and destroy the causes of sickness, poverty, discord, unhappiness, war, and death and reject the submissive statement of false belief where human pride, conceited in its own ignorance, claims, "That is just the way it is." We are now able to find and understand the mistakes that are causing these failures and destroy them and, in so doing, turn those desirable hopes, beliefs, and assumptions into an understood and achievable reality of continuous, harmonious Life.

The lessons and clues from failures are here for us to learn from. Failures consistently never went away by themselves in the other subjects we have mastered and have always insisted that understanding based on intelligent reasoning was the *only* way they would go away. And happily, they *did* go away. They always go away when correct understanding is attained. No guessing, no hoping, no waiting, no mysteries were ever involved in our successes; just solid, mature understanding of the facts through intelligent reasoning. With what line of reasoning do we expect this state of affairs to miraculously change in this, the most important subject of all, life, and death itself? Will we lethargically continue to allow baseless and erroneous beliefs to undermine our understanding of the universe and our lives, causing us to inadvertently extend the limited, suffering, and challenged human experience? Common sense and experience has shown us that great success and advancement has never been the reward for little or no effort to understand the issue at hand. On the other hand, success and advancement has always been the reward when greater understanding is achieved.

If our line of reasoning supporting our convictions and expectations is examined and found to contain baseless beliefs and assumptions, and it is desired to root out these causes of the seemingly endless failures and sufferings of the human experience and to further enrich and harmonize our understanding and life experiences, the reader is encouraged to press on, do the reasoning work, apply it, and gain ground in this most important arena of all, Life itself. When we have, through our own intelligent reasoning, forged a more correct understanding of the facts, principles, and true identity of our being, and with this understanding and its application reduce or eliminate the causes and failures of sickness, death, disease, age, poverty, crime, loneliness, and all other inharmonious challenges in our human lives, we will certainly be fighting and winning the battles against ignorance and erroneous beliefs. Thereby, we unveil our true Identity and have contributed to the entire victory of this, the final war in the age of reason.

Notes

- This work builds on a line of reasoning from the simplest of concepts to concepts that, although still logical and sound, will be generally unfamiliar to present human reasoning. An attempt to assimilate and apply the methods presented in Chapter 7, entitled "Application," before following through with the line of reasoning presented in Chapters 1 through 6, would only serve to hinder one's grasp of the subject. Similarly, an attempt to constructively assimilate a conclusion that A=C before the preliminary facts are presented that A=B and B=C would also hinder one's reasoning and understanding of why A must equal C. Patience is always a companion of intelligent reasoning.

- Numerous endnotes have been added to demonstrate that the nonsectarian principles and lines of reasoning employed in this book are the same principles and lines of reasoning that the origins of the world's major religions were based upon. For a broader understanding of how the principles and reasoning presented in this book relate to the ancient texts, the reader is encouraged to consult the endnotes as they appear referenced in the text. Unfortunately, the correct understanding and proven demonstrations of these founding principles have been almost completely lost long ago through tragic misunderstanding and erroneous beliefs. Nevertheless, through one's improved understanding and resultant demonstrations in the areas of health, wealth, and happiness, the principles will be proven to be one and the same. True facts never go away; they may just have been hidden for a time.

- The concepts presented herein also destroy the bedrock of many erroneous, ancient, cultural human beliefs. Naturally, these deep-seated, habitual beliefs will tenaciously resist any undermining that leads to their inevitable demise. It is for this reason that the logic utilized in destroying these tenacious beliefs may be found to be somewhat repetitious but, I hope, not tedious.

Chapter 1

Are Things in the Universe Really Things?

Most scientists and astronomers estimate the physical universe started approximately 15 billion years ago in what has been called the Big Bang Theory. To the best of their knowledge there doesn't seem to be any evidence of a universe prior to the birth of ours, when an incredible explosion took place known as the Big Bang. After the initial explosion, the Big Bang has expanded and is continuing to expand and evolve now and into the foreseeable future. Recent findings suggest that the expansion of the universe is actually accelerating due to, it is believed, a force called dark energy that accounts for approximately 70 percent of the universe's mass. It is also believed that another "dark" constituent, dark matter is an invisible structure that seems to connect the galaxies, and this dark matter accounts for another 25 percent of the universe's mass. The visible and substantial matter that we are familiar with in stars, planets, human bodies, etc. is believed to account for the remaining 5 percent of the universe's mass.

Prior to discovering that the universe is actually expanding at an accelerating rate, most scientists and astronomers believed that the universe would simply expand outwardly due to the initial Big Bang explosive force and then eventually collapse back together again due to the attraction of gravity all bodies impose on one another. This would suggest that the birth and death of the Big Bang universe could be a repetitive process in endless birth-death-birth-death cycles, like a weight in harmonic motion at the end of a spring expanding and contracting repeatedly. However, after combining the most recent discovery that the universe is, in fact, expanding at an accelerating rate together with the fact that stars and star-forming entities possess only finite lifetimes, it seems the Big Bang universe will eventually burn out to lifeless, cold cinders and ashes blindly hurtling into the abyss. Clearly, it would suggest that the birth-life-death cycle we are all familiar with on a more personal human level also applies to the entire Big Bang universe itself; it was born, has a limited lifespan, and terminates in death. The death of the universe will not take place anytime soon. Although our sun has an expected lifetime of 10 billion years, the majority of stars, red dwarfs, have life expectancies of 10 trillion years, one thousand times longer than our sun. Therefore, the universe, at 15 billion years old, is quite young, much like an infant.

For our Big Bang universe, many theories postulate that the nuclear fusion reaction of the stars utilizing the lightest elements of hydrogen and helium (which seemed to be formed near the beginning of the Big Bang) are the source of all heavier, visible elements that then coalesced and gravitated into a seemingly infinite number of planets, asteroids, comets, and particles with which we are familiar. We know for sure that one of these planets has also evolved plants, animals, and human beings from these resultant elements.

However, the actual details and theories about how the material universe may have evolved are of no real consequence here. The important fact is that the universe we are aware of is here now and we are in it, now. No mere theory about that fact, for we are here in this universe right now. Surely the phenomena of what seems to be a physical universe did take place and there is no question that it did considering the enormous sensory evidence we have supporting that observation. Clearly the logical place to begin to understand the universe and everything in it is to reason about the very phenomena we observe before us.

As it is accepted that the phenomena of the physical universe did occur, questions as to its origin and nature have been going on for as long as rational thought has appeared in it. Questions like, What caused the universe? Is the phenomena of the universe a cause in and of itself, or has something else caused it? If caused by something else, what is that something else? How was all this accomplished? Further and probably the most important question after all these technical ones is: Why did it happen? Individuals in the fields of science and theology have been grappling with these questions for centuries.

Understanding empty, three-dimensional space

To begin to answer these questions, let's reason about the most elementary concept or phenomena of the so-called physical universe. I call it a "so-called" physical universe because the reality of an actual, physical universe comes into serious question later in this book, but for now, it will be treated as our familiar physical universe. For the purpose of analyzing a physical universe, there doesn't seem to be any concept in it more elementary than empty, three-dimensional space. All phenomena consisting of matter, planets, stars, dark matter, dark energy, radiations, etc., in the physical universe, including our bodies, resides in this singular space or volume. We and everything else move around in it and share this singular space. Therefore, the first and most elemental concept to analyze is empty space with nothing in it, just the concept of three-dimensional, empty space.

At first glance, an empty volume of space containing no other phenomena surely seems to be "nothing." However, just considering empty space by itself, some facts are evident in our present sensory experience. Although not a solid, matter related "something," it still seems to be an actual, physical thing: a single volume, a single space, a single entity in which all other things like the things of our Big Bang universe are placed. Pretty important stuff, this nothing space thing. We can observe that the phenomena of a physical, three-dimensional, empty volume is certainly there and within the volume itself among other observations, we can project an infinite number of points, lines and planes that also have an infinite number of relative positions with each other. So, for a "nothing," as empty space would seem to be at first glance, there is actually quite a lot going on there. In fact, after briefly studying it and describing it, a pure, empty volume of space is actually quite a complex concept. Therefore, because of the seemingly physical presence of three-dimensional space it can hardly be viewed and described as "nothing" and definitely must be viewed and described as "something." A "nothing" would be no concept at all. Therefore, empty space has all the properties and characteristics of a physical "something." It is there, it is a phenomenon, and in this respect it is very similar to all the other more commonly known physical phenomena that empty space envelopes like galaxies, stars, planets, dark matter, dark energy, etc. All seem to be physical, objective phenomena and all seem to be objectively "there" or "out there" as the case may be.

Continuing the reasoning process, the following questions could now be asked: How could this phenomenon, this "something" of empty, physical space come into being? Did it require a cause or source of origin? If so, what is its cause or source? Is it really a physical, objective volume or some other entity? Whatever it is, did the phenomena of empty space cause, create or express itself? Although it is seen to be a phenomenon, that is, a "something", could it have been always "there" like some kind of a fixed entity throughout eternity?

It has been shown that an empty volume of space is a rather complex concept and that it is "there," an effect, a phenomenon. The line of reasoning utilized here insists that the only entity or medium that can conceive of, cause or create any concept, phenomenon or effect, anything that is "there," can only be that entity that can think, and thinking of course, is the only process that can conceive of any concept, phenomenon or effect. Of course, the only entity that possesses the ability to think is mentality, consciousness or mind. (In this book, the terms mentality, consciousness, mind, soul, life, and intelligence are synonymous terms and are used interchangeably to describe that entity that has the ability to think, conceive, believe, know, understand, etc.)

"Thingies" are ideas, not "thingies."

Therefore, is it logical to assume or believe that the effect of empty space was always mysteriously there without a specific thinking cause or source of origin, or even more ludicrous, can an empty volume of space, that is just an effect, cause and create itself? If so, by what logical means? Does physical, empty space have a mind of its own with the ability to think and say to itself, "I can think and therefore I can conceive of and create myself as the effect of empty, three-dimensional space?" By logical definition, an effect cannot cause an effect. Having no mind of its own, it is obvious that the effect of empty physical space could not conceive of, cause or create itself by itself and go on to become an empty volume of space. If it is assumed that empty space, that is just an effect, was always there without a cause to think of and conceive of it, this too would be illogical because empty space is clearly an effect and an effect must have been caused by a thinking, causing entity preceding it. Therefore, it cannot be assumed that the effect and phenomena of empty space was always there without a cause, and furthermore, its cause, whatever that thinking entity is, must have preceded it, or at least, is primary to the effect of empty space in a cause/effect relationship. And that effect-generating entity preceding and causing the effect of empty space can only be mind or mentality, the only entity that has the ability or creative power to think, conceive, cause, and create any effect or phenomenon. Furthermore, the only "effects", the only "phenomena", the only "concepts", indeed, the only "thingies" that thinking can create are *mental ideas*. Therefore the effect of empty space and any other effect or phenomena in our entire conscious awareness must all be mental ideas created by a thinking entity, consciousness. This particular point that <u>all</u> phenomena are, in fact, entirely mental ideas, mental "thingies" with no objective material reality, ever, is paramount in this line of reasoning and must be found reasonable to the reader or, at least, under serious consideration, if the reader desires to correctly understand what is presented in the remainder of this book.

Fundamental cause of empty space

It was shown logically that the so-called physical effect of empty space has no mind of its own and therefore has no ability to think and conceive of or cause itself. It could not have always been there of its own accord without a specific thinking cause preceding it. It follows that some thinking entity prior to it must have caused it. The so-called objective phenomena of space is certainly there, if not an almost infinite amount of it in the so-called physical universe. As stated earlier, the line of reasoning utilized here insists that the only entity that can conceive of or cause any concept or effect that are ideas, can only be that which has the creative ability to think and thereby conceive of and cause the subject ideas. And, as stated earlier, the only entity that can think and conceive of any idea is mind or consciousness. It is noted that the only *offspring* that a thinking mind can have are ideas conceived of and held within that mind. Therefore, empty space is the idea or offspring and consciousness or mind is the sole cause and source of this or any other idea, effect or phenomena. Nothing else can think of or conceive of an idea except mind, mentality, consciousness. So it is seen that empty space did not cause itself, was not always there, and that it is an idea that must then be the offspring or manifestation of consciousness or mind, the only reasonable creator or source of all ideas, effects or phenomena. To believe without intelligent reasoning, that is blindly, that the rather complex concept and idea of empty space that is seen to be an idea, a phenomenon to be sure, was mysteriously always there without a specific thinking cause is illogical and does not stand up to common sense reasoning. It surely is an idea just like all the various phenomena of dark energy, dark matter, stars, planets, and atoms are also ideas and effects and must have been caused at some point in time just like the Big Bang theory and common sense agree upon. The answer to "what is" and "where is" this creative cause, this creative consciousness that thought of and conceived of the idea of empty space and the rest of the things in it is discussed in a later chapter in detail.

Location of space

The next question in our reasoning could be, Where is the actual location of this idea, empty space? Is it out there residing as physical space somewhere out there in *more* physical space? To assume that the idea or effect of empty space, that has been reasoned to have been caused and created solely by consciousness, now resides somewhere "out there," outside of consciousness as a real physical, objective entity is impossible and illogical. Thinking is the only creator of ideas. How does a mentally created *idea* become a physical objective idea-"thingy" outside of the thinking entity that conceived of it? How did the *idea* of empty space leave consciousness, its only cause and conceiver, and become a real physical, objective "thingy out there" external to this consciousness that conceived of it? By what mechanism or thought process did it, the *idea* of empty, three-dimensional space or any other idea or effect for that matter, leave its only source, consciousness, and become this so-called physical, objective idea-thing "out there" external to its only source? It is reasonable that consciousness or mind is understood to be singly all-powerful in regard to being the sole cause of the phenomenon, effect or idea of empty space, but consciousness and any other concept presented in this book must also follow the logic of intelligent reasoning. In the creative process, to blindly believe that consciousness simply caused an idea of actual physical space to be an actual "thingy" unto itself, that is, as an objective, physical, spatial environment "out there" external to consciousness, does not stand up to intelligent, common sense reasoning. Consciousness, the only creative entity there can be, cannot cause a physical, *objective* thing external to itself, and certainly not an actual, physical, objective thing internal to itself. These are two entirely different and separate realms, one being physical and objective and the other being mental and subjective. But consciousness can certainly conceive of or cause ideas and effects that behave and seem to have all the properties, all the traits of physical, objective things that are the subject of its own thinking.

Please note that in this book, the terms *subjective* and *subjectively* refer to ideas and concepts held within consciousness and nowhere else, while the terms *objective* or *objectively* used in this book refer to so-called actual, physical things believed to be within an environment that is physical, outside of and external to consciousness. These "objective phenomena" are believed to have their own separate objective being and substance that is external to consciousness "out there" in a so-called physical realm.

Linking consciousness, the only cause that can conceive of any idea that is its effect, with actual objective physicality that is something totally unlike the nature and realm of consciousness, is a feat that logical intelligent reasoning will never allow. Blind, baseless and *unreasonable* beliefs may allow the "reality" of consciousness, or some other mysterious and unknown power to create a real, objective, physical, material universe, but intelligent reasoning cannot. Intelligent reasoning is the only process useful and acceptable here if we want to succeed just as it has always been in our past endeavors to gain greater understanding in uncovering erroneous beliefs no matter how comfortable and cherished these illogical beliefs may seem to be.

Even though we can conclude through sound reasoning that the phenomena of so-called physical space never left its only source, consciousness, the seeming appearance and phenomena of so-called objective, physical space and all the things in it still has to be explained in detail and accounted for. After all, the seemingly physical, objective universe with all the things and phenomena in it including us and our bodies certainly "appears" to really exist as real "thingies."

Universe of mental phenomena, not "thingies"

The only way consciousness recognizes or acknowledges the effect of so-called physical, objective space, as an actual, physical entity unto itself, is when it is presented as a mental phenomenon, as an idea within consciousness subjectively where this idea possesses all the properties and characteristics of an objective, physical-space-entity. A great example illustrating this we experience all the time in our own dreams while sleeping. It all seems to take place in an objective space or spatial environment, and it all seems very real and genuine at the time demonstrating that so-called physical phenomena are, of course, nothing but ideas residing in individual consciousness while sleeping. Therefore, the conundrum of objective physical space, while appearing to be an actual, objective thing "out there," but is not in reality, is simply explained as an *illusion* of actual, objective, physicality taking place in but only one way, as ideas in consciousness, the only "place" there is. But even an illusion must be an idea or an effect because the illusion is there subjectively and therefore must be supported by the idea of it, just as the subjective experience of objective phenomena in dreams are supported by ideas in consciousness while we are sleeping. Therefore, what seems to be real and actual, but is not is simply experienced as that of an illusion or, more correctly, an illusion-idea. It is called an illusion-idea because the phenomenon of empty, physical space must be an idea in consciousness, but to be viewed as real physical space it must be a hypnotic illusion believed to be true because it has been shown that physical, objective space is impossible. Empty space is an idea that resides in consciousness, but space as a real, objective thing can never exist - anywhere.

When we start to consider that our entire objective, solid "thingy" type universe is actually mental phenomena held in mind, we get our first glimpse at the incredible and awesome creative power of consciousness. We begin to see that only baseless assumptions and superstitions without the application of intelligent reasoning can believe in the objective reality of an actual, physical universe that seems to be separated from and residing outside of consciousness. The day is too far spent in this age of reason to sit back and blindly concur with baseless assumptions, superstitions and mistaken beliefs of objective reality when intelligent reasoning clearly reveals otherwise. How long do we hold on to our baseless beliefs and insist that Earth is flat before we consider the urgings of intelligent reasoning?

Seeing should not be believing

Just because the phenomena, effect, or idea of physical empty space appears and is apprehended and experienced even knowingly as a subjective idea, does not automatically imply that this idea of physical space must then be a correct, true and valid idea. In like manner, just because $2 + 2 = 5$ has an appearance on this page (that, by the way, must be occurring subjectively in consciousness for both you and me) as an idea does not make it a correct idea just because it has made an appearance and entered our awareness. Even though "it is there", we know it is not true. So-called physical, objective space can appear to be real in only one way. Just like dreams while sleeping, the answer "5", Earth is flat and a pencil in a glass of water is bent can appear to be real in only one way— as a mistaken idea, an illusion-idea supported by an erroneous but temporary belief in it being true. Even though it is nothing but a wrong idea, if mistakenly believed to be true, failures and limitations will ensue as they always do as a consequence of utilizing erring, blind beliefs and wrong answers rather than actively knowing the intelligent facts and truth about an issue. Therefore, it is correct and stands to reason that the appearance of so-called actual, physical, objective empty space is nothing more than a false belief subjectively experienced. It is a hypnotic illusion when the subjective idea or mental phenomena of empty space (in consciousness, of course) is erringly believed to be real, physical, objective space "out there." This is the only way a false illusion-idea can ever be conceived, manifested, and apprehended, and that is when it is supported by an erring belief and conviction that it is true, the same as any hypnotic dream state portrays.

Therefore, the entire volume or space of the universe is not a physical volume as an actual objective entity, but is the subjective idea, the mental phenomenon or effect of empty space held in and maintained by the only entity that can conceive of, think of, create, maintain, locate, recognize, be aware of and communicate anything - consciousness. Subjective consciousness is the only "place" there is, and actual *objective* phenomena external to consciousness is impossible.

Granted, at this point in our experience of empty space, it may seem to make no difference whether it is thought to be a physical, objective thing or a subjective idea or effect in consciousness. However, it will be seen that making the distinction between the two is a very important one. It will determine what cause is and what is mere effect and what is fact and what is merely blind, foundation-less belief that, if left unchecked, can produce dire consequences of untold misery and failure. Any endeavor utilizing errors instead of facts will always be fraught with "issues." Mistakenly believing $2 + 2 = 5$ while building a house will be guaranteed to produce various failures and problems in its success and enjoyment.

Material things residing in space also untrue conclusion

Now that the concept of empty space has been reasoned upon what it is and its logical origin and location, the next group of phenomena to consider are the "material things" that reside in empty space making empty space no longer empty - the entire universe we now *seem* to be living in. The same reasoning process for analyzing empty space is used to analyze the material things in it. Because it has been reasoned that the empty space phenomenon, although holding all the properties of objective physical space, must simply be an idea of empty space held in consciousness subjectively, it can hardly be assumed or believed now that the objective material things in this subjective idea of space are anything more than ideas - mental phenomena and effects as well.

Based on the same reasoning process that empty space can never be an actual, physical, objective entity unto itself but is only an illusion-idea of these parameters and characteristics, so too the material things in it can never be actual, physical, objective "thingies" unto themselves. Like the empty space idea and effect, material things are also simply ideas, mere mental effects that possess no substance, consciousness or thinking ability of their own to communicate, report or transmit any kind of data whatsoever. They too can only mistakenly appear to have this ability as an illusion or a dream but are still mental phenomena or ideas occurring subjectively within consciousness. All shape, form, texture, force, weight, inertia, velocity, color, pain, pleasure, properties, characteristics, etc defining all objects and phenomena in the universe can only be in the family of ideas residing subjectively in consciousness just like all the parameters and characteristics of empty space were. Again, objective "thingies" are translated to subjective ideas. These ideas define all the characteristics, properties and relationships of all the subject visible material phenomena and non-visible phenomena like dark energy, dark matter, fields and radiations, etc., that make up the universe. In order to be created, revealed, known, recognized and possess data describing structure, shape, color, texture, action, feeling, pain, pleasure, quality, harmonious or inharmonious conditions, etc., requires that all phenomena containing this data must be ideas, simple or complex that must reside subjectively in consciousness.[8] There is simply no other place for any idea, effect, phenomenon, thing, concept or illusion to be thought of, created, reside in, possess being and be recognized - other than in consciousness.

Although in the past we believed things like dark energy, dark matter, planets, stars, light, radiation, various fields, human bodies, etc., to be actual, real, substantial, physical, objective entities and things, just like we believed empty space to be an actual, physical thing, we find out through sound reasoning, that both so-called physical space and the material things in it are simply illusion-ideas, mental phenomena falsely believed to be real objective physicality whose objective reality cannot stand in the light of intelligent reasoning. [9]

To erroneously believe and conclude that we consist of real, objective matter and that mind or consciousness resides in the finite idea of organic bodies in physical, objective space is applying no more effort to understanding the facts of our being than that of stone age superstitions and unenlightened, ancient beliefs. Just because the illusion of a physical, objective universe is a very good, a very detailed, a very large and a relatively very old illusion has absolutely nothing to do with the validity of its reality when examined with intelligent reasoning. All illusions, simple or complex, large or small, new or old, obvious or not, are fake and unreal and the only reality they can claim is that of a dream, like all illusory, mental phenomena projections occurring subjectively within consciousness. Of course, dreams and illusions vanish when we awaken and see they are not true reality. So too will all these false, illusory phenomena of a material, objective universe vanish when we truly understand the reality of their false nature.

Another approach illustrating the falsity of a material, objective universe is as follows. If a material, objective universe does not consist of immense, complex ideas residing only in consciousness, but is outside of and separated from consciousness and is now out there as the material, objective universe that we are familiar with, the material, objective universe would cease to be and cease to be apprehended. The only entity that can apprehend anything is consciousness and consciousness can only apprehend ideas subjectively within itself. If it were an actual, material, objective universe and not a complex idea as we have concluded, by what means of communication or awareness could there be between consciousness, which can only know ideas, and a material, objective universe that has no consciousness to think, say or communicate anything, like "Here I am and these are my details of existence"? By what communication process could this take place within reason without the action of ideas and thoughts held totally within consciousness? But, you may ask, what about the five human senses?

False testimony of the so-called five human senses

Through logical reasoning, all of the so-called objective universe consisting of space and the material things in it are simply ideas or mental phenomena and effects subjectively residing in consciousness and can never be actual, physical phenomena or objective reality - only as an illusion possessing these particulars. The ideas that compose the universe are generated, held and maintained in consciousness and even though our five believed to be "physical" senses and their respective organs boldly testify to the reality of physical, objective phenomena, they too are reasoned and understood to be only hypnotic illusion-ideas as well. We erringly believe that *so-called* physical, objective eyes testify that it all certainly looks to be a material universe, that physical ears concur that it certainly sounds like a material universe along with the physical nose that it smells like one, the physical mouth that it tastes like one and the whole physical body in general that it certainly feels like one.

Although these various sense testimonies seem to be very convincing, they are still all based on the flimsy erroneous belief of an objective, physical universe. It is believed that these "physical" organs are real entities outside of consciousness containing communicating mechanisms capable of formulating and reporting sensory data via so-called "physical" nerves to your so-called "physical" brain where this sensory data now mysteriously jumps out of the "physical" realm into your consciousness, your conscious awareness. How this mysterious jump of data is made between the so-called physical brain and conscious consciousness is never quite explained in detail and never will be because it is an impossibility based on an illusion of real objective physicality erringly believed true.

Our cultural beliefs commonly hold and argue that we experience an objective universe through the physical senses of sight, hearing, smell, taste, and feeling. This would be a reasonable argument when based on a real, actual, objective, material, physicality (that can never be), but falls apart when intelligent reasoning rules objective, material phenomena and sensory organs of the body to be out of the realm of objective reality and into the realm of subjective mental illusion-ideas and effects occurring within the mind. The various organs we erroneously believed to be the instruments of the five senses have no real being, no physical objectivity, no sense-ability, no mentality and no intelligence of their own, nor do the various ideas and phenomena they claim to be "sensing." All phenomena, including eyes, ears, nose, etc., and the "thingies" they detect are subjective ideas residing in consciousness and can never be outside of consciousness having separate intelligent ability or communicating processes of their own. Reason informs us that only consciousness can have any intelligent ability to think of, conceive of, create, know of, sense, communicate and recognize ideas and report data. Ideas (and illusion-ideas) are the effects, the "playthings" in the sandbox of consciousness, the only cause, and ideas can have no intelligence, physical objectivity or thinking ability of their own outside of consciousness. There is simply nothing "out there" and certainly nothing out there that can interact materially with so-called organs of sense. Only in a hypnotic dream of illusions can so-called objective eyes, ears, nerves, etc., that are all just subjective illusion-ideas themselves, seem to possess independent thinking ability and have the intelligent power of reporting data about even more so-called material, objective "thingies" out there. However, these activities, the intelligent sense-abilities of seeing, hearing, feeling, smelling, etc., certainly do exist as true ideas and faculties and are to be utilized and enjoyed. But they can only exist subjectively within consciousness, the *only arena* possessing the intelligent power to report, process and enjoy any idea. These good and enjoyable faculties were never dependent on make-believe "physical" organs, only in erroneous, dreamlike illusions.

The baseless, belief-testimony that a real, material universe is a fact, can no longer stand as an actual fact or the truth of being in the light of this intelligent reasoning. Only consciousness can think of, conceive, maintain, and recognize all ideas subjectively within itself—even illusions and dreams that claim other realms of reality like a universe made of objective space and intelligent matter, must still reside in mind.[10] To wrongly assume and believe that ideas and effects, that can only be held subjectively in consciousness, can somehow migrate through some mysterious process and miraculously become actual, physical, objective, matter-phenomena outside of consciousness and go on to interact or communicate with consciousness via the five physical organs of sense, is an illogical conclusion destined to the "Earth is flat" trash heap. Logically through intelligent reasoning we must inevitably always conclude and understand that consciousness is the only creator of any idea and the only location where any idea, dream, effect or illusion can reside, be recognized and have any conscious activity.

Awesome possibilities

Therefore, the entire Big Bang physical universe phenomena or effect and its continuing evolution right up through and including physical human beings, are all illusion-ideas or simply mental phenomena subjectively residing in consciousness. Although these ideas do seem to exhibit their own individual material characteristics, laws and properties as when we thought they were actual physical entities unto themselves capable of communicating these details, we can now begin to understand that all these things can only be in the realm of consciousness and are all simply occurring as subjective illusion-ideas in a hypnotic dream because objective physicality is impossible and must be an illusion. Again, we begin to glimpse the awesome creative power of consciousness. An analogy here could be a very sophisticated, interactive movie about a so-called physical universe, a virtual reality if you will, that is being experienced in the theater of consciousness, the only creating, living and experiencing medium there is. Previously, to believe in the so-called infinite, material universe was awe inspiring enough, but to now begin to see it all was generated by and resides *within* consciousness as ideas *and* that we are consciousness too - now that really starts to suggest some wonderful and awesome possibilities that will be developed later on!

Coming "back to Earth" however, the illusion of a so-called physical, spatial universe made of separate bodies with finite forms, material substances with various and mostly negative qualities does however, seem to define and envelop our present experience as humans in a so-called objective, physical universe. And it is here, only in the imaginary illusion, effect and dream of a so-called objective, physical universe where all the wrong ideas and actual failures of suffering, violence, and death, and the like can occur - if we allow them. But we are starting to understand they are occurring only in a dream, in a mental, subjective illusion. Wake up from the dream, and the illusion of wrong ideas, limitations, and failures will cease to be as well.

We begin to suspect and see the advantages we could have if so-called objective physicality is nothing but a false idea, a falsely believed subjective illusion similar to a dream held in consciousness and not a physical reality at all. We can now ask, how rigid then are the supposed laws, characteristics and properties of so-called physical matter if these very so-called laws and properties and the so-called matter they govern are just ideas residing subjectively in consciousness with no reality, no law or objective substance and presence unto themselves? How real and reliable then is the testimony of the five senses? Are we still bound to believe and be subject to these supposed laws and properties of "objective nature" that are now seen to have no status of being "real things", possess no intelligence to report any data, and yet seem to cause so much suffering and failures in "nature's" physical universe?

Universal consciousness is single and alone

When looked at in this light of intelligent reasoning, it can be seen that consciousness is the only entity there is and is all-inclusive. Consciousness with its thinking ability is the only creator or cause of ALL ideas (ideas being effects which are also synonymous with phenomena and illusion-ideas in dreams) and this consciousness is also the only "place" where an idea, effect and illusion can reside - including an entire universe! *Therefore, consciousness is the only entity that has "being" and in this sense it is universal and totally alone.* Being the only entity in existence this universal consciousness is absolutely by itself and is singular with no peer. Correct ideas, effects and mental phenomena along with false illusion-ideas that can define an entire objective universe, have absolutely no mind, thinking ability or intelligence of their own.

For these reasons of consciousness possessing the *only cause* and the *only place* where any effect can appear, universal consciousness is all one being, one entity and is truly alone.

All phenomena and effect, true or false, fact or hypnotic illusion, are conceived within, reside, and are known and recognized within this consciousness, the only entity there is. Space and matter are seen to be ideas only, residing as phenomena within this consciousness and are not external places and things containing intelligent substances as formerly believed. It must then follow that this universal consciousness, this *only* entity in existence, must be the *only* substance there is, if anything is to be called a substance. Where we once believed in things as having and being real substance, we find that they were, in fact, believed illusion-ideas exhibiting all the characteristics of physical space and material substances, but can only come into our experience subjectively as ideas or mental phenomena in a dream within this universal consciousness. This universal consciousness must then be the only real substance or medium there is. Therefore, the nature of the belief that things and phenomena are made of fixed, physical "stuff" or substance, is the same as the erring belief that Earth is flat - both seem to have an appearance but both are false. We find after careful reasoning, that all these physical things and phenomena are really ideas, not physical objective things, and are made of and reside in the only true and real substance in existence, universal consciousness. The reader is cautioned that this reasoning does not deny *the idea and meaning* of things and a universe, but it does deny the existence of objective, material, physical things and an objective, substance-universe. All "things" still exist and have an identity but are now correctly translated into subjective, compound *ideas* in the medium of the only entity there is, universal consciousness - and have never been separate, physical, intelligent "thingies" outside of consciousness. The true and detailed identity of all things and phenomena is preserved as the illusion of objective, physical things and phenomena are accurately translated into the correct concept of mental ideas residing in this one universal consciousness. Likewise, Earth did not lose its true identity when it was translated from a flat floor to a sphere or from a geocentric to a heliocentric concept. We simply came closer to understanding Earth's true identity that was always there.

Therefore, when we mistakenly believed the testimony of our five so-called physical senses as to the actuality of real physical space and the material things in it, it was simply an act of mistakenly believing in an illusion. Actual so-called physical phenomena outside of consciousness and possessing intelligence simply cannot exist as a reality although it may appear as if it does to our deluded senses residing in the hypnotic dream. Remember, these are the same unreliable senses that, once upon a time, boldly proclaimed Earth to be flat and the floor of the universe or that a straight pencil in a glass of water is bent. Based solely on our untrustworthy senses, our conclusions and beliefs of a physical universe are incorrect and have been fooled by the illusion that, although these ideas including our bodies and sensory organs do behave *as* physical things and space, they *can never be* actual physical things and space in a real physical environment outside of consciousness. And they can never possess a separate consciousness outside of the only consciousness there is, the one conceiving universal consciousness. Perhaps this universal subjective illusion of a so-called objective universe could be called the mother of all holograms. Our so-called physical senses are always deceiving us; railroad tracks merge in the distance, the sky touches Earth in the distance, and of course, Earth is flat. All of this false testimony would be believed to be true were it not for our intelligent reasoning correcting this mistaken sense testimony.

Erring beliefs cause failures and vulnerability

Because it has been reasoned that the universe and our entire experience of it occurs within consciousness subjectively and not outside of consciousness objectively or as actual physicality, our entire individual experience can vary tremendously depending on our own individual conclusions and beliefs of where, who and what we think we individually are. True, clear and correct conclusions always yield harmonious and beneficial results as opposed to erroneous beliefs. We have been forced to learn this principle all of our human lives. For example, attempt to balance a checkbook or build a house while believing $2 + 2 = 5$ and then do it with the true fact and conviction that $2 + 2 = 4$. The former will of course result in endless, inharmonious failures while the latter will yield a successful, harmonious result. This negative result-mechanism or negative feedback-mechanism of failures occurs automatically when we are utilizing false, erring "facts" we believed to be true instead of the true facts. This principle operates in every facet of our lives. The negative feedback-mechanism results of so-called failures, problems, sickness, disease, confusion, suffering, and limitations are all very familiar to us but their true cause and solution in every case, is not. We will see that not only are false beliefs and concepts the root cause of so-called failures and problems, but the root cause of so-called sickness, disease, confusion, suffering and discord as well. As in all endeavors, understanding the facts specific to each erroneous belief will undo or heal this so-called failure or discord that the erring belief has caused, and thereby regain harmony, the true nature of life. We will see that failures, problems, sickness and discord are "so-called" because they are not real or fact and their only source is not some mysterious power beyond our grasp, but simply a mistaken belief or erring assumption that believed it to be true, nothing more. We will see that these failures and limitations never came from any other source other than a mistaken belief and we will see that it is as simple as that.

When we believe the illusion of physical reality to be the real facts of our existence, that is, to be real, objective entities unto themselves containing separate forces, laws, consciousness and thinking ability outside of universal consciousness, we automatically place ourselves in that false dream. With this erring conviction, firmly believed to be true, we are then forced to conclude that our lives and minds must be contained in, depend on and somehow consist of separate so-called physical, intelligent bodies capable of reporting pain, abnormal functions and conditions that are also believed to reside in a physical universe and be subjected to all the inharmonious material laws, limitations and rules therein. Naturally, accepting and believing these erroneous, material concepts will bring a sense of vulnerability because all the failures and limitations are now possible in this illusory, dreamlike framework.[11] Firmly believing in this false illusion of a physical "reality", you will now seem to consist of a limited and challenged physical body that must obey the laws and consequences of a physical, material universe and world. Not being aware you are actually in a subjective illusion or dream, threats to your material body and well-being will be taken seriously and experienced as real. In this erring conviction, various levels of fear will continually rule every moment of your life, for your life is now believed to be dependent upon, and consisting of a so-called objective, physical body in a physical environment with all its potentially harmful and dangerous "laws", "rules" and "properties." Believing we all are material organisms that must die someday or that you have contracted some sickness are both examples of either subtle fear or excited fear, respectively. Subtle fear expects the negative "real" consequence to inevitably occur in the future but is not overly focused on it, while excited fear sees a negative "real" consequence as a present threat immediately occurring now.

Correcting erring beliefs

On the other hand, when awakening from this false dream that is actually a nightmare, we begin to understand that there is no physical reality, no physical laws, no limitations or rules "out there." It is all operating as ideas subjectively within universal consciousness. Being consciousness ourselves we must somehow be a part of this universal consciousness that is beginning to appear, as is explained later in this book. We begin to understand that through the power of sound reasoning, inharmonious failures and discord can be changed to success and harmony in *all areas* of life, not just the more common failures we are familiar with. Through reasoning and understanding the true facts that effects can never be outside of consciousness possessing separate thinking ability or intelligence, we are now able to override and supersede these negative and harmful so-called laws and failures with authority and confidence. The previous sense of vulnerability and fear that was naturally felt when so-called physicality and its laws were believed to be true will subside and be replaced with a wonderful sense of power and fearlessness because you will begin to understand that there is no physical, objective truth or laws carved in stone - only subjective ideas in consciousness.[12] These errors and failures are subject to change exactly like the erroneous answer of 5 can be rejected and changed with intelligent reasoning, and success is enjoyed.

Instead of the commonly held belief that we are objective, material beings living in a material universe, we now find through intelligent reasoning, that the entire universe, composed only of ideas and possessing no separate intelligence, actually lives in us, subjectively in consciousness, the only intelligence there is.[13] When this point is understood and proven through your actual demonstration of harmony over discord, one of the major battles in the final war against erroneous beliefs will be won.[14] We simply need to be aware of and understand the true state of our being through intelligent reasoning and apply it to the erroneous beliefs that falsely claim and manifest otherwise.

Chapter 2

Consciousness

For some, Chapter 1 may have brought a whole new and expanded meaning to the words consciousness and substance. Through intelligent reasoning free of baseless dogma and blind, material beliefs, it was established that universal consciousness is the only player, the only entity, the only creative engine *and* locality of existence and being - the entire universe as defined by every idea and illusion-idea there is. It was reasoned that this universal consciousness must be the only substance and the only medium that can conceive of and maintain all ideas or phenomena, true or false, that envelope the entire so-called objective universe including our mentalities and bodies. All cause and its corresponding effect - ideas and illusion-ideas - must reside within consciousness as there is no other medium, substance, entity or place.

Because consciousness is the sole source and location of all effects and concepts that are mental ideas, consciousness itself cannot have nor reside in a finite form. Form is just another idea and an idea is something that consciousness conceives of or "manufactures" and can never be what consciousness or intelligence itself is, or is housed in. Even on the human belief level of life, one would find the task of describing the form or outline of consciousness impossible. It has no form because there is nothing preceding the only cause there is to conceive of a form. *Formless,* universal, consciousness itself is the first and only cause that has the power to conceive of all idea-phenomena. And whatever the phenomena are that compose and define our universe; whether they be space, shapes, forms, colors, galaxies, planets, stars, people, emotions, passions, pains, pleasures, trees, flowers, facts, illusions, etc., they are all communicated as ideas (or illusion-ideas) and for this reason they all reside within the only entity that has the energy and power to stage a mental universe - universal consciousness.

Abstract nature of universal consciousness

In the past, human beliefs have always associated consciousness with its respective, personal, physical body and brain as in the case of a human being with its seemingly individual mind, or for instance, a dog or a cat with its individual mind. Their minds linked together with their respective physical brains and bodies, form the various individuals and creatures we are familiar with. How do we now grasp and rationalize the concept of this formless, universal mind that holds all things as ideas (or illusion-ideas) of the entire universe subjectively without the aid of a physical brain and body? After all, we have always believed that consciousness needs an objective, warm-blooded, formed, life-support system to exist. We ask, "How can consciousness exist without the corresponding life-support system of its physical body and form?" In our present cultural belief system it seems to be inconceivable for consciousness to exist without a physical body to house it or provide it with a life-support system without getting into religious dogma and baseless beliefs which this book and intelligent reasoning refuses to do. Beliefs that cannot be supported by intelligent reasoning cannot be entertained as useful facts and must be discarded. We have blindly believed the physical universe to be a real, physical, objective entity only to now reason that it must be made of ideas only that in the case of a so-called objective universe and things, are seen to be mostly illusion-ideas subjectively held in consciousness just like dreams do. It has been reasoned that there are no real, physical phenomena or things and these "things" are just idea-images if you will or illusions on the screen of conscious awareness. Our *un-reasonable* human beliefs have it all backwards and inverted. Intelligent reasoning prohibits the actuality of objective space, matter, radiations, fields, etc. They are all ideas (generic for real ideas or illusion-ideas) within consciousness, the only entity that has the power to think, cause and maintain them. Logically, these ideas, these effects cannot possess *another* thinking consciousness because they are just ideas to begin with. Ideas solely caused by consciousness the only creator, cannot become another separate and distinct consciousness that is now believed to be housed in and dependent on a human body that we now see, is itself just an idea of finite form, density, color, texture, etc., residing in consciousness. Consciousness cannot reside nor be contained within an idea-image such as a brain or a body. The brain and body are ideas contained within consciousness and consciousness, the only cause and location of all ideas can never have a distinct, finite form of its own. It conceives of ideas and forms but can never be the idea or form. Just as it is logically correct to see that an effect can never be a cause of itself, so too an idea or idea-image like a brain can never be consciousness, the cause of the idea-image of the brain. It is an *un-reasonable* and illogical cultural belief that a life-supporting, physical brain and body are required for consciousness to exist. We must try to not sit too proudly upon that material high-tech horse and humbly acknowledge that maybe we still have a few "Earth is flat" erroneous beliefs lurking in our "advanced" society. In fact, as far as understanding who, what and where we truly are, our "advanced" technological society armed with a few computer chips and laser beams, is still at the mouth of the cave we thought we left ages ago—until now....

Oneness of universal consciousness

On the one hand there seems to be an almost infinite number of individual minds with their corresponding personal, material, intelligence-bearing bodies, and now on the other hand, we have this "other" mind, this universal mind or consciousness without a body or form, that has been reasoned to be the very source and location of, what seemed to be, an objective, physical, universe and everything in it including ourselves. How then are all these separate individual minds and this "other" universal mind related and resolved? To answer this question let's first look at and review this "other" universal mind that was reasoned to have conclusively conceived of the so-called objective, physical universe in Chapter 1. It has been established that consciousness or mind is the only engine or thinking medium that can conceive of or manufacture any idea, be it a true fact or a false illusion. Something that is not consciousness or mind cannot think of nor conceive of anything. Not only is this creative universal mind the only substance, for all phenomena, true or false, are generically ideas that are subjectively held within it and are not substance, but it also must be only one in quantity because mind, being the only and sole conceiver and locality of all phenomena must be totally alone. Mind is the only creator possible. It is second to none. Nothing could be before it to create it because it is the only creator there is. This means it was always there and always will be. What could destroy an entity that does not possess or is dependent on a material body or form? To put it another way, it must be the only entity that is, or the only thing going on - ever.

Through this line of reasoning it must be eventually understood that this single and only universal mind or consciousness is the bottom line or single, universal source and residence of all phenomena regardless of the nature or location of the phenomena. Stated another way, all being, all phenomena, reside in the very interactive and creative theater of consciousness as ideas. The ideas or effects that it conceives of and creates are only subsequent actions that reside within this consciousness. Thinking of or conceiving of ideas, true or false within itself, is what this universal mind does and as we have reasoned, these ideas cannot also be what this mind is contained in or dependent on like a brain. Mind itself cannot be an idea or in an idea but it is the only "thing" that can conceive of, cause and reflect ideas within itself. For the only thinking and conceiving element to have a form, an idea that contains or outlines it, implies another thinking element must have thought of it or, it thought of a finite form for itself and then mysteriously climbed into it, both of which are illogical and impossible. For this reason consciousness itself has not and cannot reside within a form, and is therefore *invisible* and at the same time it is the *only substance* or entity in existence and hence, its unique oneness. Being the only thinking and creative element without a form renders the quantity of consciousness to be one as it is the only entity there is and is truly alone in this respect.

Because this universal consciousness must include all phenomena, effects and existence within itself subjectively, this automatically defines the singular entity of consciousness as *infinite*. It is the only creative element, the only thing going on and there is nothing outside of it. It is simply and purely ALL and the buck stops there. The entire universe, so-called objective or otherwise, resides within it. Due to its invisible, infinite and sole nature that envelops all phenomena or ideas within itself, it must also be *indivisible.* All thinking, knowing, and feeling activities of consciousness are confined to this invisible, infinite and indivisible, universal consciousness. Therefore, there cannot be a separate, additional consciousness, separate thinking entities or intelligences, nor can there be any ideas residing outside of or in addition to this infinite and singular consciousness. It is truly alone or all one in this respect.[15]

Impersonal nature of universal consciousness

Having no form of its own, this one, universal, infinite consciousness or mind cannot be personal but must be totally impersonal because person is just a form and form is just another limited, finite idea held subjectively within mind. Even if you postulated that this one and only mind somehow through a process we are not yet familiar with, tried to break itself up into more than one mind it would still be the *only* thinking, conscious, invisible entity without a form that brings it back to being itself again, the only substance and entity there is. Mind is clearly indivisible and is therefore, still itself, always complete, one and in full communication with itself as one infinite being. Consciousness is therefore, impersonal, infinite, invisible, and indivisible and can never escape nor separate itself from itself, cannot enter into and reside in its ideas or effects, nor can it ever divide itself into more than one singular being, itself. By this reasoning, mind or consciousness is totally one, a singularity that is impersonal, complete, invisible, indivisible, infinite, and therefore alone (all one).

Phenomena of multiple minds

Because of the reasoned, innate oneness of universal consciousness, there can be only one way in which the phenomena of so-called additional, separated, multiple minds and thinking entities that somehow reside within bodies that we are familiar with, could seem to take place. The *impossible* phenomena of multiple, separated minds occurred in the same way that the so-called objective, physical universe occurred, that is, as a false, hypnotic illusion. All hypnotic illusions to be illusions require a firm belief in them to gain their so-called "validity" or "reality." In like manner the illusion of so-called separate, individual minds in material bodies could only seem to take place when an erring but firm belief and conviction in the illusion supports their validity and reality. Therefore, minds separated from the one and only mind are just that, a false belief or an imaginary dreamlike state that views individual minds to be within the idea, image and illusion of brains and material bodies making them capable of individual activity such as thinking, worrying, pain, pleasure, sickness, disease, abnormal functioning, etc., and seem to be separated from the one and only mind or consciousness there is. Because the whole hypnotic illusion of separate minds is logically impossible due to the reasoned indivisibility of the one and only universal and infinite mind, it can only seem to possess reality in a hypnotic dreamlike state, but it is still not the real state of affairs. How the mistaken illusion of separate, multiple minds that we are familiar with are caused, is discussed in a later chapter in much detail.

I realize that the concept of one central, universal, consciousness is quite contrary to our present experience where a separate consciousness seems to be found in all individuals and creatures. All of these separate beings seem to have finite, physical forms in which to "house" their separate minds and all seem to need material substances to sustain their lives. However, it should start becoming apparent that all these so-called physical, objective illusion-ideas and erring beliefs of multiple, minds separated from the one infinite mind and now residing within bodies and material substances are all starting to have a major validity problem. And that problem is their inability to stand up to common sense, intelligent reasoning that finds so-called real, separate, objective, minds, bodies and substances to be illusions and a farce at best. Only when it is uncovering dogmatic arguments of age-old cultural beliefs as false and need to be discarded, is intelligent reasoning interested in them. And reasoning is *especially* interested in these erroneous beliefs when, as you will see, they are found to be the very root cause of the nightmarish illusion humans seem to be trapped in - endless failures, fears, crime, drug abuse, disease, wars, poverty, starvation, sufferings, aging and death in a seemingly objective physical universe.

Thinking does not originate in a brain

Because infinite mind is the only entity in existence, the entire universe itself - space and all the things in it - reside subjectively in this mind as a compound *idea* very similar to a dream confined within one's mind and experienced while sleeping. Cause, that is mind, and its effects that are forms, so-called substances, events, feelings, etc., that are the ideas of this mind, must reside within this one impersonal, infinite substance because nothing else has this power to manifest ideas - there is simply nowhere else to "be." Being the one and only, *infinite,* consciousness in existence, it must also be the *only single life, being or soul* that can exist and experience living. In fact, it is the very same singular consciousness activity or life activity that is now reading this page (you) (which page is residing subjectively in universal consciousness as a finite idea) as the one that wrote this page (me) even though it appears that we are separated minds with separate individual bodies at this time in our respective illusions. The consciousness aware of the idea of this page at this time is not the separate life or distinct consciousness that we believe to be dependent on, and somehow living within the objective illusion of one's brain since there are no actual, physical, objective brains to generate or locate consciousness. The only consciousness that can be aware is the universal consciousness, *infinite* and *one*. As we have seen, all phenomena including a brain are merely ideas, dreamlike phenomena, and consciousness and intelligence cannot dwell in ideas, in dreamlike phenomena. But the whole concept - the erring idea and belief of one's mind contained in and dependent upon a brain certainly dwells in consciousness, the only media where all ideas and beliefs are located and exercise activity.[16] There are no actual physical brains that generate conscious activity but just very good illusion-ideas or hypnotic effects shadowed forth as so-called objective brains (but still *subjectively* within consciousness of course). Brains are not made of an actual substance, so-called objective or otherwise. Brains cannot have the ability to think because they do not possess the necessary substance required for thinking to occur. They are just mental ideas and images thought of, formed, and residing subjectively in consciousness, the <u>only substance</u> that has the ability to think.[17] Impersonal, invisible, indivisible, and *infinite* consciousness is the only entity that is, and is also the only entity that is able to think and contain all phenomena. It is the only single entity that can be conscious, think, know, and feel anything and all this thinking, knowing and feeling activity, is life itself. It is the only cause and effect of anything. It is the "all" of life, nature, the cosmos, or whatever you wish to call it. We are all "it" right now but must obtain a greater understanding of this fact if we are truly able to see "it", live "it" and enjoy "it" eternally.

Life experienced as blackboard or movie screen

All so-called finite, objective phenomena like physical space, planets, galaxies, radiations, fields, separate brains and bodies, etc., are simply illusion-ideas held within this one mind like complex mental phenomena but still have no substance, life, being, awareness or consciousness of their own. Mind is infinite in every measure of the word except quantity, where it is the one and the only substance or being that is. It is the only energized place where creation, life and awareness can exist. Without consciousness and its inherent power to think and create, nothing is.

Consciousness or mind can generate and cause true ideas and mistaken illusion-ideas depending on if the thoughts forming the ideas were based on intelligent reasoning or blind, erroneous, beliefs. Consciousness in its manifesting power is like an infinite, impersonal blackboard or a movie screen where any idea can appear or be expressed, right or wrong, true or false, reality or illusion. The blackboard itself, like any blackboard (or movie screen if you prefer), is neutral and does not know nor care what appears on it. Its only purpose is to accurately provide a neutral medium or a playing field on which all ideas or effects, right or wrong, facts or illusions, can be expressed or manifested.

Impersonal Intelligence the only real Consciousness

However, on this infinite blackboard of consciousness, the only entity where both facts and illusions can be expressed and manifested, depending on their correct intelligent or erroneous belief sources respectively, only facts and their intelligent source can be real. Erroneous beliefs that generate and support hypnotic illusions on that blackboard are simply mistakes and cannot also be real. Intelligent consciousness and its ideas alone must be the only reality because it can generate only the facts and the truth - ideas that are correct and real. On the other hand, mistaken illusions on the blackboard caused by mistaken beliefs cannot be real also because they are not facts, and are only temporary and fleeting errors contesting and opposing the true facts. As in any intelligent field of study, errors have no permanent standing as facts and must be simply uncovered for the mistaken impostors they are attempting to be. Reason concludes that this one and only impersonal, universal, consciousness, soul or life there is, must be intelligence, must be alone and must generate and cause nothing but correct, factual, intelligent ideas on that blackboard. Sourced from intelligence, these ideas must be of perfect, good and harmonious quality. Therefore, impersonal, infinite, universal, intelligence being all there is in reality, is defined as all cause and all effect occurring within its own infinite oneness and it can only know perfect and good ideas generated within itself - intelligence. Putting it another way, intelligence is simply being aware of what it itself is because that is all there is in reality; one impersonal, infinite life, one soul, one universal consciousness where all its ideas are infinite, correct, perfect, harmonious, good and are manifested on that blackboard as a universe of itself for there is no other life, being, intelligence or entity.[18] Intelligence is the sole Principle of Life.

Impersonal consciousness, mind, intelligence, soul and life are all synonymous terms and can be used interchangeably for this single, infinite, alone, mental entity. Also from here on as appropriate in this book, those terms that belong to, or are associated with the one, impersonal and *true* Consciousness in reality that is infinite and perfect Intelligence, are capitalized to eliminate being confused with a *false and imagined* consciousness based on mistaken beliefs. The qualities of perfection, goodness and harmony, etc., are the only qualities that can be assigned to any idea Intelligence has generated. To say and believe that Intelligence can conceive of incorrect, inharmonious, imperfect and not good illusion-ideas is illogical and can no longer be called Intelligence but is back to being an unreal, imaginary, erroneous belief-based consciousness. As will be shown, the course of our everyday affairs bears this out.

Considering the omnipotent nature of universal consciousness

It has always been quite amazing to view the immensity of the so-called material universe. Just the seemingly infinite size of it and the immense variety of planets, substances, and living organisms stretch and dazzle the imagination. As an example of this immensity, if our sun was the size of the period at the end of this sentence, our Milky Way galaxy alone, just one of untold billions of galaxies, would be the size of the United States. Impressive illusion! Lots of so-called "stuff" and "space" out there! And this is just the counterfeit version of the REAL UNIVERSE.

As discussed previously, human beliefs have attributed the origin of the so-called objective universe to the material Big Bang theory. However, these dogmatic beliefs have major disconnects in their reasoning where missing links of logic leave us hanging in the lurch. For instance, what caused the Big Bang and what was before the Big Bang? More specifically and keeping within the bounds of common sense and intelligent reasoning, how exactly was so-called objective matter, space and consciousness created? We can say that matter is really energy in a different format as described by Einstein's famous equation but that begs the question, where then, did the energy come from? We never seem to be able to put our arms around and feel at ease with the explanations and conclusions of the far-reaching human beliefs grappling with the origins and substance of an objective, material universe. When getting right down into the weeds of the question, "How do so-called objective things become thingies "out there" floating around in another objective thing that is empty space?" no reasonable explanations are offered and we say a Big Bang or supernatural cause did it. We simply don't know the details down in those weeds. There are uncomfortable blank spots in the reasoning along with baseless and dogmatic concepts containing unresolved guesswork and mysteries that we just can't get our arms around logically. In this respect, a material universe residing objectively outside of consciousness will always carry these inherent mysteries as fantasies and illusions always do.

On the other hand, compare the concept of a so-called material universe to the idea that the entire universe and everything in it are really idea-phenomena subjectively residing in consciousness. Instantly we are more able to apprehend and put our arms around this conclusion because something that is happening in consciousness is an inherent environment of our life, being and experience. We dwell in consciousness and its ideas 24/7 even while sleeping. It is really the only "place" where we ever will live and experience life. We feel more comfortable with the reasoned explanation of a mental universe in that we are inherently much more familiar with the creation and interaction of ideas than we are with the not-so-familiar "creation" of so-called objective, physical space, matter and energy out of thin air whose origins remain unexplained in the Big Bang concept and others.[19] Feeling more comfortable with a more familiar "mentally created" universe where only thinking and ideas are involved without the ominous origin-of-objective-thingies-problem, we can also have a better appreciation for the awesome, infinite power and all-inclusiveness of this singular consciousness that envelops all. Definitely something to think about when you consider that we are expanding and adding an entirely new dimension to the term we called life and consciousness, that we now begin to see, is enveloping the entire universe within itself. We begin to see that we do not live as isolated organic beings but that our life and entire being actually resides in an even larger life; in a living, thinking and infinite universal consciousness. Everything from the smallest subatomic particle to super cluster galaxies reside in one, living consciousness as ideas even if some of these ideas may be temporary illusions at this time. What was once dead, cold space containing mindless matter is now living ideas and phenomena within a singular living consciousness. We find we are now on the same playing field with this newly reasoned creator, the field of thinking, ideas and understanding, truly a field of intelligent life. A universal consciousness that holds the entire universe within itself as mental idea-phenomena is more awesome, alive, powerful, secure and loving than we could ever imagine with a cold, material, objective, dead universe created in violence, mystery, and dogmatic guesswork of the Stone Age.

Illusions can appear but are unreal in an infinity of real facts

It was reasoned that universal consciousness, the only entity there is and contains all, is infinite. Being infinite also suggests that this consciousness can also harbor infinite erroneous beliefs that seem to be real (if mistakenly believed), as well as infinite, intelligent facts that are real. Although never real, it is noted that mistakes can be as eternal as facts are. The war between what is versus what isn't can go on as long as mistakes continue to be erroneously entertained as facts or truth. However, even if an infinite amount of errors can seem to be generated, appear on that neutral blackboard or movie screen and are hypnotically believed to be true in one's life experience, they are still unreal and imagined illusions. Only Intelligence and its infinite, factual ideas on that medium are real, and infinite Intelligence, the only true entity there is, knows no opposition. For example, does mathematics know of an actual, real opposition when five is expressed as the sum of two plus two? There are no separate entities or powers in reality opposing the true, correct facts but only temporary and erroneous beliefs, mistakes and assumptions. Intelligence being the only, true, infinite entity in reality also implies that any other separate "intelligence", mind or life can only be *imagined* non-intelligence. This imagined, separate "non-intelligence" and its unreal, false ideas are always represented or projected as the finite, inharmonious illusion of a so-called objective universe and all its challenges expressed subjectively on that impersonal blackboard of consciousness. This is the case because their basis or source is outside of and separate from the one true reality and therefore must also be unreal. Infinite Intelligence contains only true, real, factual and harmonious ideas. It stands to reason that any so-called "idea" in addition to the *infinite* quantity of true, real, harmonious ideas must be *false* and *inharmonious* because they are separated from, additional and are outside of this *infinite harmonious* quantity and quality.

Because impersonal Intelligence must be infinite due to its singular nature of being all that truly is, its factual ideas must be infinite as well. The process of this awareness of itself to itself (for there is no other self) must unfold endlessly and go on in a forever "now", that is just another way to describe the concept of eternity. After all, it is infinite and its self is the only self there is. There can be no other offspring of Mind, of Intelligence, but its conscious idea of itself, an infinite idea constantly revealing the effects and awareness of its celestial self.[20] Being an infinite Mind necessarily requires that its conscious idea of itself, the only Being in existence, must be infinite as well. Finite illusion-ideas manifested as separate, finite material bodies and objective things are through this reasoning, ruled out as unreal illusions. Also, infinite Mind and its ideas that are infinite does not need to conceive of nor create any new ideas, for that would imply incompleteness within an infinity. Infinity, by definition, cannot be incomplete.

To put a finer point on it, impersonal, infinite Intelligence does not really create ideas but simply *reveals* the ideas of what it already is as the truth of its infinite self to itself. Would it seem logical that $2 + 2 = 4$ needed to be created, ever? For all of us, it just was revealed as a true fact without any requirement that it needed to be created. It was revealed as a true fact that was always there throughout eternity. Reveal is also a better term than create because create seems to imply a creator as being separated from its creation that was reasoned to be a false belief, whereas the term reveal implies the true state of affairs; an unfolding awareness of itself to itself as all there is in reality. Also, the word create seems to be linked to the mistaken belief of a material, objective universe where it seemed that material substances needed to be materially created along the lines of a timeline that the Big Bang Theory suggests. On the other hand, when the entire true universe is seen to reside in and be the self-awareness of one, single, timeless, celestial Mind as an infinite quantity of revealed ideas of itself that always were there like $2 + 2 = 4$, then the word reveal is again, more appropriate than create.

We begin to understand that all effects, like our so-called material body and the space it resides in, can only be conceived by and reside in consciousness as ideas and that these effects can never possess any separate intelligence or being of their own to report data like thinking, sensation, abnormal or normal functioning, etc. We begin to see they are simply mental effects being revealed subjectively within consciousness as mental phenomena or ideas and now we can learn to control them.

As in all other arenas where we have been successfully engaged, understanding the truth of the matter always enabled us to control the outcome to our advantage. In like manner, the increased understanding that you will have after uncovering, battling and destroying various, erroneous beliefs with intelligent reasoning, will always yield more harmonious experiences and less failures for you. Also in like manner, the yield of increased harmonious experiences will always be in direct proportion to the level of understanding you possess and apply, just like we have already demonstrated and enjoyed in the many other arenas residing in the realm of consciousness. They all operate and obey this same principle of intelligence.[21]

Chapter 3

Identity of Impersonal, Perfect Intelligence

It has been reasoned that the only entity in existence is impersonal, infinite, universal consciousness that can conceive of ideas or cause effects, as either intelligent facts or erroneous beliefs. Also, this impersonal, universal consciousness is the only medium, like the neutral blackboard or movie screen analogy made earlier, that can manifest *all* ideas and effects irrespective of whether they are true ideas or false, hypnotic illusions. *All* effects can only be ideas. And they can only reside subjectively within universal consciousness itself, making that universal consciousness the only substance, the only entity, the only place, the only cause and the only effect there is. Every thought, place, shape, color, property, so-called space and matter, i.e. all phenomena of the universe - are ideas that can only reside in this singular consciousness. It has also been shown that the true nature and quality of this consciousness, this sole cause and its only manifested effect - must be that of Intelligence alone. Intelligence alone can generate only true, factual ideas and knows nothing about illusions and erroneous beliefs for these phenomena or ideas are simply *mistakes about the facts* and have no more basis in reality than 2 + 2 = 5 does.[22] Impersonal, infinite Intelligence is shown to be the only entity in existence and is invisible and indivisible as well. Being the only consciousness and Intelligence there is, implies it must be the only awareness and this brings us inevitably to the conclusion that it must also be the only Life, Soul or Ego as well.

Infinite Ego the only presence and the only body

Being the only Life, Soul, or Ego, it has been reasoned and concluded, that it must be invisible, indivisible, singular, complete, and alone and that these characteristics simultaneously make this one Being impersonal and infinite. Not infinite in time and space. Time and space are simply more finite, objective, illusion-ideas formulated in a limited, belief consciousness. But infinite in the sense that it causes and contains *all* within itself and there is simply nothing else. It is the only thing that is. There can be nothing in addition to or outside of an *infinite all*.

Even the belief that time is a real entity is an illogical conclusion. As an example, neither our human sense of being nor any other sense of being or awareness, true or false, can ever leave "now." Now will always be now and to escape from now would be impossible and illogical. We can remember past ideas and wonder about future ideas but all activity of consciousness will always find itself inescapably locked in now. We will see that the "now" we always find ourselves in, is eternal having no beginning and no end and we were always there, in the "now" throughout it all. The seeming march of time with its constantly changing evolution of birth-death cycles will be shown to belong in the entire erroneous family of hypnotic illusions of finite, objective space, matter and organic life.

Concluding that this universal and infinite Intelligence must be the only Life, Ego, or Soul, it is for this reason of infinity and it being the "only", both in cause and effect, which makes this indivisible entity a unity. Being the only Ego there is, when it senses, that is, understands its idea of itself as itself (being the only true idea there is, as there is no other idea to sense, be aware of or understand), it observes that it is the only presence, the only power, the only quality, the only Life, the only Ego, the only Identity, and the only awareness of its infinite, intelligent, individual, perfect self. The awareness and understanding of the subjective details and ideas of itself are manifested, expressed and known as the only body or universe there is in reality. [23]

The only Life there ever has been or ever will be boldly declares, "I AM! I AM all! I AM unity. I, Intelligence, am the only presence, knowledge and power. In other words, I AM the only cause and principle of real ideas that compose the universe and my conscious awareness and understanding of these ideas of my Being is my infinite body, the universe, the only *man*ifested effect whose quality of being is always perfect, eternal, harmonious and good." [24]

The "I" in "I AM" is perfect Intelligence or Mind and is the only true cause. The "AM" in "I AM" is the harmonious and perfect effect or idea within Mind that this Mind is aware of and is the only true universe in existence. In this system, I AM defines the infinity and unity of all that Is - Mind conscious of itself as the only universe of true ideas. "I" can never be without "AM" for a cause cannot be without its effect and vice versa. Individually understanding these true ideas reveals an infinitely, complete and whole universe. "I AM Life, Intelligence and the only Ego. I AM the only Identity and Being that ever was or ever shall be and I eternally feel the perfect feeling of love and joy of this realization. In this infinity, I AM YOU and YOU ARE ME in a singularity of perfect Being—RIGHT NOW!" [25]

Universal creative law of cause and effect revealed

From the above reasoning emerges the most important universal law of creativity. Succinctly, mind and the universe it causes and manifests is always one being - and that universe is always the exact image and likeness of the individual mind that created it. Individual mind is the only energy or power that can cause any effect and this effect or idea is always reflected or expressed exactly in detail as an entire universe of itself. All effects are always directly and exactly linked to their cause. As we shall see later, all concepts of mind, whether correct or in error, will always follow this creative law and will always cause and manifest its own universe as the expressed image and identity of itself. In fact and although it does not look like it right now, you, the human being reading this page *are also* the entire universe you believe your personal self to be residing in. You are always the individual mind *and* the individual universe that your mind has caused. "I" is always identical to the "AM" it creates. You are not *in* the universe; you *are* the universe. All universal phenomena and of course, your life experiences are one and the same and are the expressed image and likeness of you. Whether in truth or in error, I will always be AM.

Of course, all of this is quite a stretch from our human beliefs as to what constitutes life, the universe and what the individual ego and body are. Human beliefs correctly locate ego as consciousness or mentality, but we also believe that this separate and finite ego, this life, this identity, this intelligence of ours resides in and is dependent on a so-called physical body and brain that resides in a physical universe. [26] How and where this ego, this life, dwells within the body and brain is never quite firmly and scientifically established except by blind beliefs. These beliefs really start falling apart when one dies, the body and brain are still there, but the ego, life and intelligence are nowhere to be found. The explanation of where the ego or life now resides after dying is contained in even more baseless and ludicrous beliefs regarding their so-called "afterlife" or that life is simply snuffed out as the dead body seems to testify.

Individuality expanded

We see that the objective, physical universe is not what it appears to be, and serious, intelligent questions have been raised as to its validity in its so-called objective format. However, you cannot at the same time lose courage here, draw a line, and declare, "Do not let this reasoning process go any further and bring my own ego or individuality into question, because it is starting to look like I may perish and lose myself to this impersonal, infinite, universal consciousness thingy." If ever there was a place in one's life where it is necessary to have an open mind, this is the place.

Individuality and your identity are neither lost nor diminished when we reason through this issue, but rather, are gloriously expanded. You will always be aware of life as a conscious, individual self and ego but not as a limited, separate ego somehow mysteriously locked in a finite material body ticking off the clock in a birth-life-death cycle as it marches towards its inevitable demise seeking an eventual release from its material bondage. All that you truly love and enjoy now will be preserved if they are right, that is, if they are compassionate, kind, loving, and intelligent. After all, it is ALL your entire perfect, eternal universe to begin with! Human individuality is awakened from a finite dream of itself to find itself an infinite Being and Identity as one, whole impersonal individual instead of multiple, finite, personal, separate, physical individuals and identities in the human belief-dream. As in all awakenings, we sense our wakened state to be the reality and where we have always been, the dream notwithstanding. Would we rather know and live life as the Identity of one infinite Ego, secure in eternal Life and perfection as one impersonal, celestial Being; an infinite universe containing and knowing all good, or as the identity of a personal, finite, human ego laboring in a meat-sack body restricted and threatened by physical constraints and heading to a very undesirable and uncertain end of all so-called organic life?[27]

Nature of universal Intelligence and the only Ego

What must this infinite, individual, universal Life and Intelligence be and include? Thus far we have seen that the one, infinite Ego is indivisible and is all. Therefore it must be the simultaneous Ego or Soul of all. In an analogy of the awareness of a human body, a human can observe its hand as an attribute of its body, its leg as an attribute of its body, its toe as an attribute of its body, etc. These are all various bodily attributes that seem to be the human being at this time in its present human experience. Remove one attribute and it no longer possesses a whole body. In a similar fashion the infinite Ego is all separate, individual ego attributes combined as one individual Ego and Identity whose idea of itself is manifested or expressed as a whole and complete universe, its very body.[28] Remove a single individual consciousness or ego and the infinite Ego and its body are no longer complete nor infinite and therefore, the omission of a single individual is impossible.

Another useful analogy would be a hologram or DNA molecule where all segments or fractions of the whole, contain all the data of the entire hologram or DNA molecule within themselves. In like manner the one, infinite Ego and individuality is aware of Itself as the combined ego or whole meaning of all. The infinite, one Ego is the combined consciousness of all humans, male and female as one, the combined ego of all animals male and female as one, the combined ego of all plants, male and female as one, all soil, all rocks, all planets, all stars, all galaxies, all super-clusters of galaxies, all atoms, all electrons, all anti-matter, all radiation, all space, dark matter, dark energy, etc., etc and even life forms we are not even familiar with yet as the one, singular, infinite, Ego and its universal body.[29] The soul or consciousness of all entities falsely believed and subsequently portrayed erroneously as separate, finite, creatures and physical things residing in their entire physical universe, are really one Soul when correctly understood. All souls or minds, when wakened out of the illusion on planet Earth and elsewhere, are then simultaneously aware of *Itself* as the one and only Being, individual, universe and Identity there is.

When these facts are reasoned through and are understood, each individual will still know and feel like an individual just as the individual knows he or she is an individual now, but obviously on a different scope. The awareness of an impersonal, infinite and singular Being that is always whole, perfect and harmonious will be vastly different from the erroneous, finite, personal, imperfect, inharmonious, separate, human-belief awareness of i am a human being (lower case intentional).

One Ego, individually known as I AM

In reality, my I is your I, my Ego is your Ego and my Identity is your Identity but *only* in the sense that we are identifying our true self and are aware of our true self as the singular, impersonal, infinite, Ego; as the only Intelligence, the only individual, the only Being there is. This correct understanding of Self and Ego is not the erroneous, personal, human-belief of a separate self and ego that, in its own make-believe dream and limited awareness, erringly harbors false beliefs, opinions, guesses, and thoughts that are then shadowed forth in its so-called separate, individual, material, self and the objective universe it believes to live in.[30] When this correct viewpoint of oneness is reasoned upon and fully understood, we can all say, "I AM" and understand and be aware of our impersonal self as the only I, the only Life and Identity, the only unity there is.[31] Our awareness will simultaneously be understood to be the only knowing, the only body and the only universe there is, was, or ever shall be and is always infinite, perfect, harmonious and existing in the infinite Now of Eternity.[32] Not in time to come or in time past but *now*, the only time there will ever be. I AM will be understood to be the only fact, the only truth.[33] I AM the only Being and the only individual. I AM the only Identity and the only Life. I AM the only cause whose *man*ifestation is the only body or universe that exists. I AM will be found to be more perfect and complete than a human could ever imagine in their present erroneous, human-belief dreams of being separate, personal, individual egos with their respective material, finite, personal bodies that is generally, the present awareness of mankind.[34]

So-called finite, material body was never required

When understanding some degree of the oneness of Being, we can speak of this oneness in the first person where appropriate. Therefore, when looked at in this light of my one, true, whole, celestial Being, what need would my impersonal, infinite, Intelligence and my infinite, celestial body of awareness have of a thinking mechanism (erringly believed to be a separate mind ego generated by and somehow residing in a brain) when the very Identity of me is infinite, eternal, invisible, Mind and my self-awareness thereof? In fact, what need would I even have of thinking, an activity that only sorts and sifts correct ideas from erroneous ones, when I already know and AM aware of all as myself and AM perfectly good and entirely settled on all questions?[35] What need would I—impersonal, infinite Intelligence—have of the finite march of time that gauges the evolution and progress of the human ego's struggle for the true facts and perfection when I already know and AM all truth and perfection?[36] What need would I—impersonal, infinite Intelligence—have of personal, finite senses and their material expressions (eyes, ears, nose, mouth, and nerves) that in a very limited way for humans seem to sense seeing, hearing, smelling, tasting and touching, when I already know and AM aware of (senses) all? What need would I—impersonal, infinite, Intelligence—have of personal locomotion (legs and feet), when I already AM everywhere as my own Identity? What need would I—impersonal, infinite, Intelligence—have of personally reaching out and handling various ideas (hands and arms), when I already have and AM all the ideas there are? What need would I—impersonal, infinite, Intelligence—have of personally ingesting, digesting and assimilating good ideas and rejecting useless ideas (digestive tract), when I already know and AM all truth with no error to reject? What need would I—impersonal, infinite, Intelligence—have of distributing good ideas and removing waste ideas from all parts of the personal body (heart and circulatory system), when I AM entirely good, circulating nothing but good everywhere, always, with no waste to ever deal with or expel? What need would I—impersonal, infinite, Intelligence—have of the personal inspiration of good ideas and the exhalation of useless ideas (lungs), when I AM already full of infinite good and inspiration with absolutely no useless ideas to deal with or remove? In general, what need would I—impersonal, infinite, Intelligence—and my celestial body of awareness have of any limited, counterfeit sense, ability, function or attribute of numerous, finite, imitation, personal, physical, human bodies and the fake, material universe they find themselves in, when I already KNOW and AM EVERYWHERE as my impersonal, singular, celestial, self, always perfect and good?

Sex and reproduction

Being one, whole, impersonal, indivisible Ego, the human question regarding the opposite sexes as being separate and distinct from one another naturally arises. From a human point of view, losing one's sexuality permanently to form one complete being could be somewhat challenging and undesirable. But isn't this oneness or completeness really what humans are seeking when, in their heart, they desire to have a relationship with another human individual; to know and feel the security, compassion, love and a sense of wholeness, completion and joy to the point where nothing else is required? A wonderful loving and secure sense of wholeness is realized when the male and female attributes are combined harmoniously as one. It is in this sense that the one Ego, the one Life having all male and female attributes combined as one is fully satisfied with an infinite sense of completion, security, joy, fulfillment, compassion and love— the actual awareness and identity of its infinite, perfect, complete self.[37] I AM is the only true Being and awareness in existence. As it has been reasoned, all seemingly separate egos or souls combined, are really the identity of one impersonal, infinite Ego, I AM, although presently our awareness of self is confined to being separate, individual, minds and bodies - finite conditions that have also been reasoned to be impossible and therefore, illusions. Simultaneously when this truth is increasingly understood, an unspeakable joy and peace that words are incapable of describing will permeate and dance throughout one's sense of the singularity of Being. Fulfillment, understanding, perfection, satisfaction, completeness, wholeness, infinite and permanent Life of the only individual in existence fills the only Ego where the only truth and the only love are found to reside.[38]

Because all finite, physicality is false and an illusion, the human's physical reproductive process is also an illusion. To believe the illusion that individual life or ego is structurally and organically dependent on physical bodies and that a new life starts with the material birth of a new human being does not in fact, add one life, mind, consciousness, or individual to the infinite all. Due to the infinite, indestructible, indivisible, whole, and complete nature of the only Life there is, a false belief of birth cannot add life or ego to the only Life or Ego there is and conversely, neither can a false belief in death remove life or ego from the only Life or Ego there is.[39] Infinite Ego or Soul is already a complete, perfect ONE, always has been and always will be. Intelligence or Ego is infinite and complete and was always this way. In fact, it was never even aware of the illusion-idea of the imaginary, material, birth-life-death cycles produced by the erroneous beliefs of human beings. Erroneous beliefs are not facts and simply do not enter Intelligence and are not acknowledged just like the mistaken answers of 5 or 7 to the sum of $2 + 2$ do not enter mathematics nor are illusions within dreams acknowledged as being a part of wakened reality.

The erroneous belief-conviction that structural, organic, objective bodies, that are only subjective image-phenomena, can create or add another life accomplishes only one thing, and that is the start of another erroneous human-belief dream wherein the unfortunate, believed-to-be, separate, individual ego or "life" is now rendered dead or asleep to the true identity of its true Being.[40] This unfortunate individual now has to painstakingly reason and work its way back to its true wakened state through all the erroneous beliefs it may now be entertaining as facts in a counterfeit, physical, objective universe including the false birth-life-death processes.[41] The process of reasoning our way out of erroneous beliefs and applying this correct understanding can occur in only one way. That one and only way is through the individual's intelligent reasoning, battling and conquering the erroneous beliefs that are harbored within that individual alone. A book or person can only explain and provide guidance to one who seeks to understand but the reasoning must be performed *for the* individual *by the* individual. No one else can do this for you. We are all alone on this one. No other way to understanding is possible or available to the individual.[42]

Erroneous beliefs regarding death

It is at this point I want to address one of the more misleading human beliefs, the erroneous belief that death is inevitable and that it introduces major changes in one's state or fortune. Death is simply another failure resulting from the erroneous beliefs that claim and argue that it is the inevitable end of a so-called physical life residing within and dependent upon a physical body, whose physical body has already been reasoned to be an illusion on the blackboard or movie screen of consciousness. The physical body is a finite illusion-idea that never had life or consciousness of its own to lose in the first place. In actuality, the only concept that can ever die is a concept that was never real - a mistaken illusion and so must eventually disappear. A concept that was never real is a false belief[43] and the false belief that consciousness or life is dependent on a so-called physical body[44] is one of these concepts that must "die." The false beliefs that $2 + 2 = 5$, 7 or 9 will surely "die" when the individual tires of the resulting failures they produce and so will it be with the false belief that life or consciousness is dependent on a physical body illusion and all other false beliefs that are manifested as inharmonious experiences. Harmonious facts (and there is no other type) cannot die and the ideas formulated within and identifying continuous and perfect Consciousness are facts as plainly as $2 + 2 = 4$ is a fact and can neither die nor be lost. As with all failures, death will no longer be experienced when its cause is understood and corrected, or more precisely, when the mistaken belief that life and consciousness are dependent on a physical body is destroyed through sound reasoning.

In addressing changes that are believed to take place upon dying, there are various beliefs surrounding this phenomenon such as one's life or consciousness goes blank or that miraculous positive or negative changes occur upon one's death, but these are all erroneous, baseless and dangerous beliefs. Dangerous for three reasons. One, because the varying beliefs in death and what happens after it are looked upon as an inevitable transition and is a factual part of "life." This blind belief does not sound an alarm that it is *not* an inevitable transition, that it is *not* a factual part of life and that it is *only* another failure brought on directly by erring beliefs in the unwitting individual's convictions. Two, the erroneous belief that death somehow automatically ushers one into a blissful life totally unlike the one preceding it fosters a lack of effort or interest by the individual to seek a greater understanding of the process. And why not? The believed blissful state will occur automatically upon dying so why give the hidden truth any more thought or reasoning effort and just be a good human being and get on with the human birth-life-death sequence? And three, that you are sentenced to some negative state that will ensue as punishment for mistakes made here and that these mistakes cannot be corrected and erased, and therefore what is the point in making any effort to avoid the inevitable results?

Life is continuous and is not aware of death or an "afterlife."[45] There is no "after" life. It is still continuous life because although we believe the so-called body seems to die, it never had an actual life to die or lose in the first place. The only death that can take place is the death and destruction of an erroneous idea or belief that is in this case, mistakenly believing life to be dependent on a material body and that this so-called body died from some objective, material cause. The only life there ever was and is still you, is the invisible, untouchable, eternal consciousness that cannot be affected or touched by any erringly believed material, objective cause or condition. So-called material, objective causes or conditions are simply erring beliefs and illusions that are residing within the only life there is, consciousness. So-called physical, objective causes and conditions are not things, they are mental illusions caused by, and are, false beliefs and convictions. These illusions can always be discarded when the facts take their place in one's convictions. Whatever convictions and beliefs one has before one goes through the illusion of a so-called death experience, be they true or false, will be the same ones present after the experience.[46] The individual may not even be aware of the specific belief of dying because he still lives and not much has changed. Life or consciousness simply and logically resumes

[handwritten margin notes: "not inevitable", "heaven", "hell"]

its awareness of its own individual convictions and beliefs whether they are tending more toward loving, harmonious, true facts and reality or towards chaotic, inharmonious, suffering, erroneous beliefs and dreams. The choice of what convictions and beliefs are reached and entertained as being true is always within each individual. The conscious experience or awareness of life constantly is, and simply goes on in a logical continuous manner no matter what erroneous beliefs or convictions contrarily testify to. There are no surprises here, miraculous or otherwise. It will always be true for each individual that what goes around, comes around. Any baseless belief that would break this logical continuity would be ludicrous at best.

Changes to one's life as a result of the failure of death is about the same changes that occur to one's life after having a cold, breaking one's arm, or having an unbalanced checkbook. Death, like all other illusory failures, does practically nothing to increase one's understanding of life or the issues at hand. As in all other failures, how much greater understanding resulted in being sick, in breaking one's arm, in having an unbalanced checkbook or any other failure we have suffered through? At best, failures can accomplish one thing and that is to demonstrate that an error exists that caused it. Increased understanding is obtained only by intelligent reasoning alone and the experience of a failure, like death, a cold, a broken arm or an unbalanced checkbook in and of themselves adds nothing, other than possibly and hopefully giving one more impetus to use intelligent reasoning to understand the true cause of the failure and correct it.[47] In fact, as in all other subject areas in our experience, until sufficient understanding and correction is reached through intelligent reasoning as to the true cause of failures and corrections are made, there is nothing to logically suggest that the failures of sickness, troubles, another death, etc., will ever stop repeating themselves as an inevitable part of our lives, even after we have erroneously believed, and lived through the failure of dying once or a hundred times.[48]

We, as humans, are actually *DEAD NOW*!

If so-called physical life containing and powering consciousness is still believed to be true, and the conscious recognition and understanding of the truth that *all* are the one, impersonal, infinite Life and Consciousness is shut out and not known nor understood, then you are indeed dead to this truth[49] and all the failures of sickness, suffering, pain, and death will continue *ad infinitum* as all false beliefs have always done when uncorrected by the facts.[50] If you, as a human being, experience death, that death will actually be a *second death*[51] because you were already dead to the truth of Life at the conception and birth of your false belief as a separate human "life" and identity. The single, perfect and eternal "I AM", continuously conscious of its infinite perfection and completeness is the only Life there is- EVER! - and is the one we seemingly and hypnotically "died away from" when the mistaken belief of "self" as a separate human being and ego was conceived.[52] Our LIFE right now, our consciousness right now can only be this ONE INFINITE AND WHOLE SINGULAR BEING, but we are temporarily convinced that our lives consist of so-called separated human egos with attached and dependent personal meat-sack bodies. When we finally understand the infinitely glorious nature of our perfect, eternal, whole and impersonal Being and Life, looking back at what we believed to be the "life" experience of the personal human being, will indeed be viewed as grotesque and pathetic walking dead! In this very real sense, we, believing to be human egos, are actually dead now and either through the guidance of trials and tribulations or through the discipline of wisdom and courage, must painstakingly reason our way back to, and reawaken to our perfect oneness of Life, the only Soul there ever was.

Life is preserved

All individualities in the universe are preserved. They, as one Being always were one in Consciousness (although erroneously believed to be numerous, separate, reproduced egos with respective, separate and finite, material embodiments) and always will be as one in Consciousness. No separate entity of consciousness "dead" or "alive" in the so-called formed, objective universe is dead, lost, left out or too insignificant for they are all collectively the one universal, impersonal, infinite, celestial Consciousness that is already a fact. It has never been an issue of changing anything real to be included in this one Being for *all* have already been included there in reality, born or unborn. Rather, it is a question of becoming *aware and awakened* to this great fact in the face of erring beliefs, dreams, and false testimony to the contrary.[53] Intelligent reasoning is our only key to this wakened awareness.

Attributes of universal Intelligence

All positive and good attributes of all individualities that are or have been in the illusion of the Big Bang universe, are within, actively known and experienced by I AM and I AM is aware of itself as the only impersonal Mind, Ego and Identity there is. I AM one Soul, one Life, one Universe, one Meaning, one Individual, one Identity. All of the perfect ideas and good virtues of individuality throughout the so-called objective universe are the conscious idea or self-awareness of the whole, complete, infinite meaning and identity of I AM.[54]

Examining our awareness of some of the separate and physical things and creatures we are familiar with, I AM contains the goodness, honesty, integrity, humor, patience, intelligent reasoning ability, kindness, compassion and love of a human being; the courage and strength of a lion; the nobility and stature of a horse; the loyalty, sincerity and sense perception of a dog; the independence, warmth and accuracy of a cat; the swiftness and grace of a deer; and the precision, agility and focus of a bird of prey. I AM includes the "allness" of universal space containing all good ideas; the harmony and intelligent order of the galaxies; the illusion destroying and cleansing nature of black holes; the awesome solid foundations and majesty of mountains; the nurturing qualities of the Earth and soil; the abundance, clarity, color, depth and purity of the oceans, sky and atmosphere; the variety, majesty, strength, beauty and flexibility of trees; the perfection, variety, symmetry and fragrance of flowers, the enlightenment, gravity, and warmth of the sun; the glorious promise and beauty of a sunrise and the serene depth and harmony of a sunset; the cleansing and renewing action of the rain; the refreshment of a breath of cool air; and on and on throughout the attributes of the infinite realm of impersonal Intelligence. I AM all perfect and good attributes because this is all that I, infinite Intelligence can be, can be aware of, and reveal of myself to myself as, the only Being there is. This infinite awareness of the ideas of myself is the body, the body of understanding and the only true universe of I AM. All present good and harmonious virtues identifying various seemingly separate beings, things and concepts were always attributes of the one perfect Ego although in the distorted human-belief dream, they erringly appear separated and objective and can contain both vices (more erroneous beliefs) as well as virtues.

Because the good attributes that are within the one Being are the truth of Being and are infinite, I cannot possibly scratch the surface of such an infinite theme but we all must begin with our own individual awakenings and battles utilizing the only tool we have, intelligent reasoning. Perfect, Intelligent Consciousness without a beginning and without an end is infinite and is the only truth, awareness, Being and individual in existence. Therefore we could not have ever been actually outside this one Life as we have been led to believe through the illusion-idea of so-called separated human birth, life and death. We, our *entire Being* was always there, within this Oneness as the only Identity, the only individual, the only cause whose awareness of itself is also simultaneously expressed as the only effect, the only body, the only universe there is. It is simply impossible to ever leave *infinite* Consciousness or Truth.[55] We always had our true individuality, our true whole and entire self there but it doesn't seem so when we are asleep to this truth in the severely limited, cruel, and tragic dream of the so-called separate human birth-life-death sequence.

Worthiness and continuity of Being

In this entire process of intelligent reasoning to understand the real facts of Being, we are not developing ourselves to somehow qualify or be worthy enough to be included in the all. *We all are the all already* and have always been eternal, perfect and good as only infinite Intelligence and its facts can be. Because we already are included in, and are the all, the actual process going on through our reasoning work is more of a process of *remembering*[56] our true state through sound reasoning, than it is of learning something that is outside or new to our inherent nature.[57] The failure of dying or suffering in and of themselves will never accomplish this. Failures never do. Like all failures, they can only demonstrate through their seemingly disastrous results that an error, a mistake is present and has been mistakenly utilized individually as a "fact", that is, as an erroneous belief.

When we are actively engaged in this final war in the age of reason, we are battling with our reasoning abilities to get out from under the cruel, illusion-nightmare of lies, hypnotic beliefs, illusions and mistaken identities and into the sunshine and unspeakable joy and peace of the clear facts of who and what we always were and always will be; the satisfying and secure Loving truth of our whole, infinite, complete, celestial Being, Life and Identity. Impersonal, infinite attributes, whole and complete, perfect, eternal, one infinite Life, one infinite Soul, one infinite Love, one infinite Truth, one infinite Joy and the *awareness and understanding* of I AM ALL is the only celestial Life, body or universe there IS. In a word, I AM the only Good there ever was or ever will be. I AM always was and always will be one impersonal Identity and individual. I AM unlimited, indivisible, infinite and an entirely complete, perfect Being alone with the awareness of my joyful unity and one-ness.[58] Within my Mind and awareness of all that really is, fear, heartache, pain, suffering and endless challenges in the erroneous, finite, birth-life-death illusion-ideas of separated egos and physical beings are not entertained, known or experienced.[59] In fact, I, perfect Intelligence, the only cause, was never aware of, nor did I ever create a so-called physical and separated, objective, universe and beings as my effect. My only effect, my only universe, my only body is the reflection and aware-ness of my impersonal Identity that is eternal Life, infinite Truth, and perfect Love.

Chapter 4

The Physical Universe: Cheap Imitation or the Real Deal?

Summarizing the major concepts established thus far, sound reasoning has concluded that universal Mind is the one and only Substance, Being, Individual, Intelligence, Life and Ego there can ever be. Within this solitary but whole and complete celestial Mind resides all cause and effect of itself, the only reality there is. Intelligence is the only cause or principle and the conscious awareness of its own infinite idea of itself is the only effect or manifestation, always perfect. Being the only entity or Life there is, and being indivisible, it is consciously aware of only itself as I AM because there is nothing else in existence to be aware of. Infinite individuality is lived and enjoyed as one individual. I AM all, I AM individual, I AM infinite, I AM Intelligence, I AM perfect, and I AM endless, continuous Life, always harmonious and good.

The body of universal Consciousness

All Being is known as and within I AM. One complete Mind or Soul aware of only one infinite, perfect idea - its consciousness of itself that is reality - the one and only Real Deal. This awareness of the infinite idea of itself is the infinite *man*ifestation of Intelligence and is the only body of understanding, the only universe, the only individual, the only Identity or conscious Being possible. I, the only indivisible Ego in re-ality, am the one and only substance and my attributes have only one quality in existence - perfection and goodness. Whatever I, infinite Intelligence reveal as more attributes of myself to my individual self as the conscious idea of myself throughout eternity (the forever now), can only be perfect, harmonious and good for that is the absolute, sole nature, quality and quantity of me.

A contrary universe and bodies

In addition to the indivisible celestial Ego that correctly knows and senses itself as I AM and contains all Intelligence (cause) and ideas (effects) within itself as the only Being and Identity, absolutely the "only thing going on",[60] we, as separate human egos and organic beings have an awareness through our sensory perception of something else going on. A so-called physical, objective universe containing many separate things and phenomena like galaxies, stars, light, planets, radiations, gravity, plants, animals, people, etc. All "things" within this so-called objective, physical universe are framed in a space, matter and time envelope where all have a beginning as a birth, followed by a life span and are inevitably terminated with an inevitable death and annihilation. As stated earlier, these finite phenomena or material "things" are called illusion-ideas because it has been reasoned that space, matter and time that envelope separate, finite forms with a less than perfect and good quality cannot be reality and must possess the nature of unreality like a dream or an illusion in a hypnotic state. What is more important and of especial concern here among all these "thingies", are a huge number of separate, individual, organic, human egos and identities existing on planet Earth that either have, or are presently heading towards their inevitable death as well. Of course, other galaxies and solar systems could contain even more separate egos at differing stages of evolution than ours but are also going through these same processes of being born, maturing and dying. All of these finite, physical phenomena appear quite contrary to what has been reasoned to be the only universe and existence in reality - an infinite unity of Being. One complete, eternal Ego - I AM - consciously aware of my infinite and perfect attributes. So what's up with this physical, objective universe with untold billions of individual substances, stars, planets, minds and creatures destined to tragic life and death cycles?

Because the singular Intelligence is the only Mind that can conceive of and maintain correct and harmonious ideas that are the subjective reflections and awareness of itself as the only universe and Being, what could possibly have been the method and motive in conceiving of the awareness of an inharmonious, objective, physical universe totally unlike the only universe in reality?[61] Before us we have a physical universe of immense space containing a seemingly infinite number of separate ideas - matter-substances, radiations, galaxies, stars and planets. And on one of these planets - Earth - plants, animals and human beings reproduce, live and die in endless cycles. Instead of one, infinite, whole, singular and eternal I AM, that has been established as the only Ego and Life whose individual awareness of its idea of itself is the only Identity and universe possible, we have an individual awareness of a compound illusion-idea containing an immense number of rational egos and identities, both alive or who once were on Earth, not to mention what may have happened on numerous other ego forming planets "out there." Furthermore, this compound illusion-idea of an objective, finite, physical universe then goes on and frames these separate ideas that seem to possess physical characteristics with inharmonious, material laws that dictate untold suffering and limitations in seemingly endless, finite birth-life-death cycles. And as if that wasn't enough, the quality of the "life" portion of that cycle, especially for the rational ego, is to "live" in its respective meat-sack, organic, material body in a physical environment while contemplating and suffering through a fair amount of violence, hard work, poverty, starvation, natural disasters, confusion, wars, terrorism, crime, aging, disease and death to name just a few. Even the separate illusion-ideas of galaxies, stars and planets are all locked in this same disastrous birth-life-death cycle as well. Where did this inharmonious illusion-idea of an objective universe with separate egos and identities come from? Why and how did this illusion-idea that always has suffering, death and annihilation as its goal, come into being?

Let us step back and look at that sole creative, thinking process again, that singular entity of universal consciousness and its ideas. It has been reasoned that the only activity that this entity, consciousness, can engage in is a thinking process. Thinking is the only activity and avenue that can lead to the formation of ideas, and all effects including "thingies," true or false, fact or illusion are always ideas. Isn't it true then that if consciousness is not acting or thinking intelligently with accurate principles and facts but is carelessly "guessing" with false beliefs and erroneous assumptions - is not really thinking intelligently at all and as a result, failures, mistakes and illusions can appear? Consciousness in this respect is analogous to an infinite and neutral blackboard or movie screen where any answer, right or wrong can be expressed granting it a presence or an appearance. Our lives are filled with devices and media capable of expressing incorrect, false data and illusions. Another analogy are computers where we are aware of the possibility of a dubious output in the contemporary phrase, "garbage in - garbage out." Maybe the best analogy familiar to us today would be the images on a movie or television screen where their mere appearance obviously does not guarantee accurate facts and authentic reality. In all examples, erroneous answers or manifestations can have an appearance and a presence, but as we have reasoned, a mere appearance does not automatically mean they are true or possesses reality. Prior to accurate reasoning we believed so-called physical space and the things in it to be reality consisting of actual, physical, objective phenomena. Judging solely by their appearance we erringly concluded and assumed the universe to be a real physical place and substance, a so-called reality containing life entities that are dependent on so-called objective physicality until they die. Only through intelligent reasoning do we now see that it is not physicality or forms containing and sustaining life at all, but merely illusion-ideas subjectively held in mind, the only "place" where life, ideas, illusions and thingies can be known and experienced or "lived."[62] Just like the mistaken calculation $2 + 2 = 5, 7$ or 9 can appear on a blackboard and is rejected by Intelligence, so too Intelligence through correct reasoning rejects the appearance of an objective, material universe to be not true and unreal. Obviously if one erroneously believes that $2 + 2 = 5, 7$ or 9 is a fact and uses this so-called "fact" in balancing a checkbook or building a house, the inharmonious failures will surely testify that an error exists. The erroneous believer is now tasked with finding the root error and correcting it if harmonious conditions are desired. Intelligent reasoning also has the awesome advantage over that of erroneous beliefs in that it can demonstrate and prove its position that erroneous beliefs can never prove. For example, take two objects in one hand and combine them with two of the same type objects from the other hand and now challenge erroneous belief, appearing as the erroneous believer, to prove that there are now five, seven or nine objects.

Cause of so-called physical, finite universe

With one *infinite,* Intelligent cause and effect in existence as the only reality, the only Being there is, the only "thing" going on, in what other consciousness did the awareness of this seemingly contrary, inharmonious, material, illusion-idea universe come from, and why and how? Where did all this space, matter, organisms and thingies come from? *More precisely, where did all these <u>false, illusion-ideas</u> come from?*

Ideas have been shown to be the essence or substance of all mental effects. Whether they are true, factual ideas with their inherent nature of Life and harmony or false illusion-ideas with their inherent nature of inharmonious sickness, death and failure, they must have come from somewhere. Obviously they are all mental effects and something mental must have caused them or established them enabling them to appear on that blackboard, computer output or movie screen of individual awareness and consciousness - one's life experience. As we have reasoned, the one and only Intelligence, the one and only Ego does not believe nor guess about anything for it already knows all as fact. It doesn't need to believe or guess anything because it is Intelligence and knows the harmonious facts about itself especially that it is the only cause, the only celestial individual, the only Life, the only universe, the only substance, the only quality and the only quantity there is.

Due to the erroneous illusion-ideas that portray a so-called physical, finite universe that reasoning shows can never be real, it would be illogical for this so-called objective universe to have been sourced from Intelligence. Still, the illusion of an objective, physical universe seems to be tenaciously there all right *and* with us and our believed-to-be finite, separate egos and bodies trapped in it! Intelligent reasoning informs us that every effect, whether fact or illusion, is linked to a generic conscious, thinking or guessing cause, accurate or not. Logically, cause and its effect are always linked as one. Something conscious and "just like it" must have conceived of it. Therefore, there must be *another* consciousness, *another* mind *and another* creator that is claiming to be *another* cause capable of projecting a so-called objective, physical universe that, by the way, has already been shown to be erroneous mental phenomena or illusion-ideas. Therefore, the only mind, ego or cause that can possibly be in addition to the one, factual, real, *infinite* Ego and individual who is the only cause and is simply all, can be nothing more than a mere *erroneous and imagined belief of a separate mind and ego*; a so-called separate cause and creator.[63] This imagined mind erroneously believes and claims itself to be *another* mind - a *separate,* individual ego, an "unthinking", guessing and falsely believing cause and creator in addition to, or to the exclusion of the only thinking Ego and knowing cause, the single, infinite Mind - Intelligence itself.[64] Of course this can never happen in reality because all has always been and always will be one, singular, *infinite* Soul and Ego, and its awareness of its only idea - perfect unity and oneness where there is *no other* consciousness, cause, or creator. But it is still reasonable that *another* mistaken and imagined mind can occur in an erring belief; a make-believe dream not based on

Intelligence or fact. We are very familiar with the expression "garbage in - garbage out"; we make mistakes all the time. On that movie screen of consciousness and life where there is infinite freedom of expression, anything is possible, right or wrong answers, reality or illusions, truth or lies, but fortunately an appearance and presence of a phenomenon does not necessarily make it real or true just because it has appeared on the movie screen of life. As the math example earlier illustrates, only intelligent reasoning can separate the real from the unreal, the fact from fiction, the truth from the lie, and prove its position. However, as with all mistakes and errors, the identification and the correction of them never happen automatically by themselves. In the realm of mind, consciousness and its ideas, (that has been reasoned to be the *only* realm), the only tool or fix available is intelligent reasoning and the application of its correct understanding to the problem at hand. Intelligent reasoning must be brought to bear on the erring belief of an additional, imaginary mind, ego and so-called thinking cause along with all its mistaken concepts and ideas it is projecting up on that movie screen of life if understanding and correction is sought to regain the harmony and perfection, that is our true Life.

Illusion of a separate, alien ego

For lack of a better term to describe this additional, imagined, mind I have labeled it the *separate, alien ego*. It is *separate* because in its mistaken claim, it wants to be *another* mind, an additional, imitating ego and to do so it must *separate* itself from the only real Mind and Ego. But this is impossible in the infinitude and reality of the one perfect Mind and Ego that is the only Intelligence and Consciousness there is. This mistaken and imagined ego is an extraneous illusion that is based on false beliefs that *separate* it and place it outside the realm of truth, Intelligence and Life where it is *unknown and alien*. Not alien in the sense of an objective extraterrestrial being who, if they exist, are not very advanced beyond us because they are still on the finite, objective level of manifestation but alien in the sense of being completely unknown to the one infinite Ego - the true facts of Being.[65] When comparing it to the only thinking and knowing Ego, cause, creator and Being there is in reality, a mistaken claim to be an additional, *separate*, outside, so-called "thinking" ego, cause and creator that alienates itself from the truth must be a counterfeit impostor, a cheap and fake imitation that is not genuine nor real, and must be rejected.[66] Naturally, the aggressive and selfish motive of this *separate*, mistaken, alien ego imitator is to have the honor of "the only creator", that it can only attempt to accomplish through hypnotic illusions because there is only one, whole and complete Ego, cause and creator that is "The Only."[67] Even with its aggressive, reckless, childish, insolent, immature, selfish, deadly, harmful, ignorant, erroneous, deceitful, and inharmonious illusion-ideas (quite a list there!), the *separate*, alien ego cannot become genuine Ego, Soul, or Intelligence. Ego, the only genuine Identity, the only individual, the only thinking and knowing cause *and* effect has already been shown to be infinite, indivisible and alone, or all-one.[68] A *separate* ego or cause in addition to the one, infinite Ego and only cause is simply impossible because no thinking, creative entity can exist outside of, or in addition to an *infinite reality* - Intelligence - that is the only thinking and knowing entity which already exists. The singular intelligent Mind is the only conceiving and creating entity there is - infinite and indivisible. Therefore, the only mind that could ever believe it is a *separate* and additional, so-called thinking, creative entity outside of the one, infinite Mind can only be a *make-believe* alien mind; an illusory wannabe, an unreal extraneous mind of vain imagination and mistaken beliefs. It and its ideas or creations can never be real, and is seen to be just a temporary illusion and dream when understood as such through intelligent reasoning that reveals this myth. This is true of all illusions and myths when the light of reason is shined in the darkness of erroneous beliefs and all the illusion-misery failures they cause on the movie screen of subjective, conscious experience vanish to their true state of unreality and are forgotten.[69]

Inevitable result of a separate cause

How and why do these erroneous ideas, these inharmonious illusions, these distorted meanings of true ideas come from a *separate*, alien ego and mind? Through reasoning we have seen that within the unity of the real, infinite Life, the only real thinking and knowing Consciousness that is the *only* cause, all ideas or effects about its universe are facts and truth like $2 + 2 = 4$, health, perfection, harmony, abundance, fulfillment, wholeness and continuous Life that cannot end nor ever be lost. Because of the *infinite* nature of true Consciousness, all true ideas or effects that exist must also be an *infinite* quantity of ideas. These true ideas and their meanings are already thought of, known and established as reality. By the definition of infinite, the quantity of all true ideas and facts are already complete and the process is finished by and in infinite Intelligence.[70] Additional, new, true ideas are impossible because infinite Mind already possesses, identifies, and is conscious of its infinite self by revealing and utilizing the *infinite* amount of true ideas and meanings in the only universe that will ever be. Also, the quality of all true ideas will always be harmonious and perfect. Intelligence knows of no other quality. The only progressive awareness of an *infinite* amount of true, harmonious, and perfect ideas can only be known and experienced as they are revealed or unfolded through *individual reasoning* where the understanding establishes a growing awareness and consciousness of the one, infinite and perfect Being, the one singularity that we all inherently are - and always have been. This singularity was also reasoned to be the only Intelligence where all ideas and meanings of its universe are harmonious and perfect. However, when a *separate,* alien mind, that is a *separate,* alien creator is erringly believed to exist, all true harmonious ideas and meanings of the one true universe will be distorted to form *separate*, inharmonious ideas or illusions that, when believed to be true, will seemingly grant the *separate* alien impostor a *separate* identity, awareness, experience and reality. Separate mind - separate ideas; separate cause - separate effects.

Creative mechanism of separateness

The imagined, *separate,* alien, so-called thinking ego can never be reality nor true Life. It can only appear as a *separate* reality or power outside of true reality making it an illusion - an appearance but no validity. This illusion of an opposing, so-called *separate* thinking creative cause, mind, or ego must now be a *separate* life and identity. It can only seem to appear this way because this erroneous point of view distorts the true harmonious ideas and meanings expressed in the one perfect universe and in their stead, shadows forth finite, inharmonious ideas or illusions that, when believed to be true, would imply that an opposing *separate* inharmonious cause and universe does actually exist. Without believing that a separate mind and its inharmonious ideas and illusions are true, the imagined separate ego and its illusions would never have a so-called life or presence. It needs blind, ignorant beliefs in its *separate mind and finite and inharmonious ideas* for it to "live." What an insidious parasite we have before us! Inharmonious lies and illusions believed to be true will automatically imply and reinforce the notion of an inharmonious, objective universe to be the fact. In a logical cause and effect analysis, this inharmonious, objective universe would also mean that an inharmonious mind must have somehow created it. Reasoning has shown that the only creative mind there is must be infinite, invisible, indivisible, harmonious, impersonal Intelligence where any non-intelligent and finite *"separateness"* is impossible.

As all true cause is solely Intelligence and the effect of its correct thinking and knowing is an infinite, harmonious quantity of perfect ideas and meanings that already exist and are complete; additional, *real,* new ideas are simply not possible in reality. Therefore, for the imagined *separate* ego to form "new ideas" in addition to the infinite and harmonious quantity of *real* ideas already existing as the only true universe, this imagined, *imposing and opposing,* so-called *separate,* thinking ego can only do so by trespassing upon, distorting and reversing already existing true, harmonious, real ideas and meanings with false, imagined, inharmonious, *unreal* ones. That of course, ends up putting forth inharmonious lies and illusions in place of the truth in its seeming attempt to validate its so-called opposing and *separate* ego and inharmonious, objective universe. From start to finish - a fantasy!

There are simply no other ideas to work with or think of in a field containing an infinite and complete set of harmonious facts and their meanings that are reality - the only universe in existence. Although claiming to be a *separate,* so-called thinking cause that is outside of the only cause, infinite Intelligence, the *separate,* alien ego has no ability of itself to think of, cause or know any original or new true idea as its own. True, harmonious ideas are unknown to the alien ego. If it did know them, it would no longer be an opposing alien impostor *separated* from Intelligence.[71] Not only does a separate ego have no real Mind status that is the only true source of real ideas, but all true ideas already are the *only* facts and are already spoken for, thought of, caused or established, if you will, by the only thinking and knowing Mind there is and is expressed as universal reality.[72] This imagined, separate ego or consciousness simply doesn't have Intelligence that is the only entity that can originate and be aware of the true, real, harmonious universe of ideas and meanings. Therefore being a *separate,* alien ego and by its very *separate,* imitating, ignorant and malevolent nature, can only cause to appear *separate,* counterfeit, unreal illusions and inharmonious ideas that are outside infinite reality. These unreal, *separate* and distorted ideas that are outside reality can only be lies about true, harmonious ideas and are really anti-true ideas if your will, because all true ideas already reside in Intelligence as the only reality, as the only facts there are.[73] The *separate,* alien ego cannot think of or cause an original idea because these ideas have already been caused by infinite Intelligence and are infinite, complete, and whole. There can never be another thinker nor can there be another creator of a reality that already is.

Because no new idea is possible or available to the alien ego, that is the so-called additional thinker, its "creativity" can only be limited to trespassing upon, distorting, reversing, counterfeiting, and misinterpreting an infinite quantity of true, real, harmonious ideas and meanings that are the only ideas and meanings that will ever be available.[74] Simply put, any creative thinking believed to be *separate* and in addition to the only thinking and knowing element there is, the singular Ego and Intelligence, will only result in *separate,* opposing, inharmonious, counterfeit illusions examples of which, I will provide shortly.

For the *separate,* alien ego, all true ideas of consciousness, identity, form, substance, and quality will be restated as *separate,* unreal and inharmonious or anti-true ideas, that is, the true ideas and meanings will be distorted and reversed as lies.[75] Due to the *infinite* quantity of true ideas describing the only universe, the alien ego has nothing else to work with but with reversing, misinterpreting, and counterfeiting these very ideas. These untrue ideas that now seem to be generated by a *separate* ego are nothing but false counterfeits, unreal, hypnotic dreams, false beliefs, lies, and illusions of the real harmonious universe. These inevitably occur as a result of the mistaken belief of thinking to be a *separate* mind - *separate* from the truth. More frankly stated, this *separate* and imagined mind is a liar claiming to be another "real" mind or cause that ends up seeming to validate its false, opposing reality, when in fact, it is all a fantasy-dream *separated from* reality.[76]

The key error is pinpointed

I realize that the mechanism and logical consequences of *separateness* from an infinite harmonious Being is being emphatically stressed here but this *separateness of mind* is the key to the illusion and nightmare of sickness, suffering, and death in the so-called human's objective universe. It cannot be reasoned about nor repeated too many times. Being outside of and *separated* (in mistaken belief only) from the one Intelligence that is the only reality, individual and Life, every idea that seems to have been "thought of" by the *separate* ego will be a lie about this harmonious truth to become the bewildered awareness of a *separate* ego and individual seeming to now "live" in an objective universe of finite and inharmonious ideas or anti-truths. Because these false ideas are not factual, that is, they are *separated* from Intelligent, orderly reality, confusion and mystification will reign if they are believed to be true as in all illusory, hypnotic states.[77]

There is only one, real universe in the theater

Universal Mind based on Intelligence is the sole cause and location of all good ideas that are facts and reality - the only universe. It is the only "thing" there ever was or ever will be and we are "there" right now even though our so-called material senses are presently testifying to the awareness of something else. There is nothing else to be aware of in addition to an infinite reality. Anything else that claims existence must be an erring belief, a mistake and an illusion. In all cases of fact or illusion however, that is, whether this mind be based on Intelligence or erring beliefs, this mind has been shown to be an impersonal entity with no form of itself but within itself is where its expressed universe, that is, where all its ideas, forms, phenomena, effects and illusions reside subjectively. Therefore *both* the true intelligent Ego and the false, separate, alien ego are impersonal, formless, invisible causes causing their respective universe of ideas subjectively within themselves - within consciousness. Their invisible and impersonal natures also requires that both, along with the respective universe they reveal, to be a singular arena of *individual* experience and awareness. Derived from the universal creative law of cause and effect, each creative ego and its respective universe is proportionally projected within *individual consciousness* as that individual's life experience defined by the predominant ego and identity in charge.

In this creative system of cause and effect, an analogy can be made between the energizing power of universal mind creating one's individual life experience or universe with the components in a movie theater. Impersonal, formless, invisible, universal consciousness, the only cause and effect entity is wholly within the theater's structure. In the theater your conscious awareness is experiencing whatever effects are on the screen. The screen is where you experience life and where your universe appears. The screen itself is neutral and unbiased and readily reveals whatever is projected upon it. The screen can never think nor create anything by itself but can only reflect or *man*ifest the effects that are projected upon it from the projector. In the same way our conscious awareness can only reflect, know, feel and be aware of the effects and ideas projected upon it - attempting to manipulate images once they are on the screen will do nothing to change or affect them. Only changes back at the projector can change and affect images on the screen of life.

The movie projector can be likened to the energizing and creative power of the one, universal, consciousness. Within the movie projector we find an intense light, an unfolding film containing data passing through the shutter and a lens to focus the subject film material onto the screen. The intense light is the energizing and manifesting power of consciousness, that singular creative mind that has neither peer nor contender. It is the only entity that has the energy and power to project, reveal and manifest ideas, good or bad on the screen. The subject film reel passing through the shutter contains the infinite and harmonious facts and meanings of Being - the detailed true ideas of the actual universe. The film reel contains the whole idea of reality and just like there cannot be two valid, whole realities, so too there can be no more than one reel of the whole, infinite facts of Being. All things in the projector up to this point - the singular creative and projecting power of consciousness (the projector light) and the harmonious truth of the one, infinite Intelligence (the film) cannot be altered as they are the actual facts of Being - the universe of reality and being seeking expression. When operating correctly, we find the sole energizing and creating power of consciousness and its complete, harmonious facts of Being projected forth upon the neutral and unbiased screen of its individual awareness as all there is. It is reality, the only universe enjoyed individually. Viewing the film correctly, that is, the projector is properly focused, we can only watch and listen to the actual facts - what has already been thought of, created and projected clearly onto the screen of individual awareness. We are the watchers, the listeners, the *man*ifested, and can never be, in truth, the creators of the film back at the projector.[78]

We can affect the focus of the lens

As stated earlier, attempting to manipulate images that are already on the screen will not change or affect them. We must get back to the projector, our creative consciousness, if we want to change any life experience. At the projector, we come to the only variable component within the projector analogy that can be influenced and adjusted to change the images on life's screen - the focusing lens. The setting of the focusing lens whether in focus or not, proportionally represents the identity and ego we *individually* believe to be - the one infinite Ego or the so-called *separate,* alien ego. In proportion to the identity we think we are, the setting of the lens will project the exact image and likeness of this setting onto the screen of our life experience and awareness - our individual universe. When accurate reasoning leads to understanding the truth that there exists *only* a singularity of universal Intelligence that is individually known as I AM - the only Ego and only Identity, the only cause and the only individual awareness of all true effects, facts and reality, the lens will be properly focused. Clearly projected on the screen of individual awareness will be the truth - an infinite, singular, impersonal, perfect, whole, complete, harmonious, celestial Being expressed as the entire true universe. It is the only Life and universe there is having no beginning and no end, is of infinite form, infinite individuality (of one Being) and is the only substance there is and is of perfect quality. On the other hand, when blind and ignorant belief claims that more than one ego, more than one thinking, creative cause, more than one being exists that is believed to exist individually as "I am a *separate* ego and identity that, in my case, is a human being - a material man", the lens will be drastically out of focus and all the good, harmonious facts of Being created and contained on the subject film will automatically be grossly distorted, reversed and upside down on the screen of individual awareness.[79] The belief of another mind, a *separate,* "thinking" mind in addition to the only Mind that exists is the only thing that can render the lens out of focus and distort the meaning of all true ideas. The screen of individual awareness will now reveal this "newly" expressed universe - inharmonious, hypnotic, belief-effects, dreams, illusions, and distorted meanings - all *separated* from the harmonious truth.

The harmonious facts of the singular, complete, celestial Intelligence and universe (true cause and its direct effect) contained on the film can never be changed for they are Truth. The meaning of the perfect, harmonious and unchangeable facts on the film however, when projected through an out of focus lens, will be reversed and distorted on the screen as the illusion of multiple, finite forms, material substances and laws and separate, personal, organic beings experiencing birth-life-death cycles that we are familiar with in the so-called material, big bang universe (lower case intentional). These distorted and false ideas are *separated* from reality and present a universe of hypnotic illusions and counterfeits on the screen of conscious awareness and are manifested all the way from super-cluster galaxies to humans to subatomic particles and beyond in both the macro and micro directions. All of these *separate* mistaken and unreal effects always begins with a birth, lives a life of limited and inharmonious qualities and always ends in death.[80, 81]

All of these false, belief-effects and illusions that are just distorted meanings of the harmonious facts of the true universe *seem to be real* and we mistakenly conclude that a material universe must have been "thought of" or "created by" something genuine, valid and real. In our reasoning, we now see that in reality, these inharmonious illusions in our life experiences are not "thought of", created nor conceived by anything. There is no other *separate,* valid, creating projector containing a *separate* film of opposing, inharmonious "facts" that define our so-called material, objective universe, but simply an out of focus lens on the only projector there is and nothing more. That out of focus lens condition brought on by the mistaken belief of being a *separate* thinking ego was the only source causing the *separate,* inharmonious, hypnotic, dream-like, illusion filled, objective universe to appear.[82]

Nature of this separate, counterfeit universe

Instead of the true, harmonious fact and reality of one infinite Ego or Soul containing all individualities as one perfect, individual Intelligence, Identity, and universe—the only cause and the only *man*ifestation—the belief or consciousness of being an imagined, *separate* ego, a *separate point of view,* can only then see and experience the distorted and op-posing lies of all harmonious facts and meanings of the *only* universe. Therefore, instead of one harmonious Mind and cause and its singular effect, these ideas will be distorted by the separate ego into separate, false concepts like believing in multiple minds and individuals and sep-arate inharmonious causes and their respective inharmonious effects. In fact, in counterfeiting the true fact of one, singular, harmonious cause that is perfect Intelligence, the separate, alien ego has, in its ig-norant opposing beliefs, splashed *separate,* multiple "intelligence" or creative causes everywhere except where it truly is. Being outside of true Consciousness or Intelligence, the *separate* and imagined, alien ego seems to aggressively claim that *separate,* inharmonious minds somehow reside in so-called material substances like a *separate* material brain encased within a *separate* material body. It goes on to claim that *separate* causes external to this mind can inflict harm on that material body and that this so-called material body, external to mind, is now an objective "thingy" that has *separate* intelligence to be able to proclaim pain and pleasure. The separate ego now knows fear as the material body that houses its mind/brain thingy is susceptible to abnormal func-tions, aging, inherited maladies, germs, viruses, diseases, inordinate cravings, accidents, bad luck, etc.

Extending beyond the illusion-idea of intelligence in a material body, the mistaken claim assigns *separate* intelligences and causes to things and places that now seem to be outside of you, outside of your consciousness and most importantly outside of your control. Examples of so-called material causes outside of you are pleasurable, habitual or escapist substances like tobacco, alcohol and drugs, your social environment like your relationships with "other" *separate* minds and egos, personal or in your workplace, your weather, your economies, your governments, your world, your entire universe.

Basically, an infinite number of separate minds, identities, intelligences and causes are believed to exist everywhere and in everything instead of in the only place it really is, in your one Consciousness, your harmonious, intelligent Mind, your I AM, the only cause, the only effect, the only place, the only individual, the only Identity, the only Being and the only Life and universe there is, forever infinite and perfect.

Instead of the true fact of one *infinite* body of understanding as the *man*ifestation of the one *impersonal* Being of Intelligence (stated in chapter 3), the belief of being an imagined *separate,* alien ego will result in the *separate* opposing lie and hypnotic illusion of objective space containing *separate,* multiple, finite, organic, personal forms and bodies. In keeping with the universal, creative law of cause and effect this entire counterfeit universe IS the whole *man* or *man*ifestation of the *separate* alien ego. Instead of the true fact of one substance consisting of true ideas that are infinite and entirely mental and harmonious as the only law, the belief of being an imagined *separate,* alien ego will result in the opposing lie and hypnotic illusion of *separate,* numerous, finite, material substances and bodies with all their illusory, untrue, inharmonious laws and properties. Instead of the true fact of one perfect and harmonious quality, the belief of being an imagined *separate,* alien ego will result in the opposing lie and hypnotic illusion of *separate* "no good" qualities all of which seem to be in addition to the already established *infinite quantity* of good, and therefore are imperfect and inharmonious.

In further examination of the real, harmonious facts versus their opposing unreal, inharmonious lies and distorted meanings, we can observe the following; instead of the universe residing in Consciousness *AS* you, as the idea and awareness of yourself and your Identity as one Being and as one universe, the belief of being an imagined, *separate,* alien ego can only suggest the lie, anti-truth and hypnotic awareness of a physical universe occupying *three-dimensional,* objective space, and you and many other separate life identities as tiny material and very vulnerable specks *in it.* Instead of an impersonal, infinite, Life that is the only substance having no beginning and no end,[83] the belief of being an imagined, *separate* ego can only suggest the hypnotic lie or anti-truth of life as finite, numerous, sentient, material substance-bodies capable of both bodily pleasure and bodily pain in finite birth-life-death cycles. Instead of infinite abundance, the belief of being an imagined, *separate* ego can only suggest the lie or anti-truth of lack and poverty. Instead of an infinite, complete and whole individual where all the harmonious virtues of male and female are combined and enjoyed as one infinite and complete Being, the belief of being an imagined, *separate* ego can only suggest the lie or anti-truth of incompleteness wherein the *separate* male and *separate* female attributes are constantly and vainly seeking union with another *separate* being for completion.[84] Instead of a glorious, perfect, complete, and whole eternal now, the belief of being an imagined, *separate* ego can only suggest the lie or anti-truth of imperfection and incompleteness where the march of time is required to change or evolve and improve its condition somewhere in the future. Instead of love and perfection, the belief of being an imagined, *separate* ego can only suggest the hypnotic lie or anti-truth of hate, fear, pain and imperfection in self, others and the general environment. Instead of one harmonious and perfect government, one intelligent Mind managing the oneness and freedom of its own infinite Consciousness, there seem to be many, *separate,* imperfect governments external to your *separate* being, that all determine and manage how much or how little freedom you shall have.

Bigoted attitude of "us and them" destroyed

This limiting and inharmonious *"separateness"* extends right down into our cultures, societies, and workings of government where the ignorant and bigoted attitude of "us and them" pervades. Instead of a better understanding of the truth we have in common within our oneness of Being guiding our motives and decisions, the corrosive "us and them" mindset constantly separates us based on man's ignorance of this truth. They erringly believe that their "knowledge" of the mind of man, the *separate,* alien mind, is all there is to work with. The "us and them" idiocy runs rampant and flourishes in *separating* age groups, gender, skin color, nationalities, religions, political parties, elitists and Joe-six-packers, "smarter" and not so smart, chosen and not so chosen, liberal and conservative, rich and poor, dead and alive, etc., that are all false illusions, images and likenesses put forth by the mistaken belief of being a *separate,* alien mind.

By reason of its *separateness,* the imagined alien mind can only ignore the true facts of the oneness of Being rendering it wholly ignorant in the truest sense of the word.

As another example, when the *separate,* alien ego is confronted with solving $2 + 2$ it will, seeing the movie projected by the distorted, out of focus lens, always suggest and argue for a *separate* mistaken idea that is always a lie and distortion as the "correct" answer and this will always result in failures when these "correct" answers are erroneously believed to be true. Uncorrected by reason, this is all the alien can see and understand. Therefore anything but 4 is the "correct" answer according to the *separate* ego that ignores the facts and believes only illusions to be true. It doesn't care what the *separate,* wrong answer is as long as it is a lie or wrong answer and will result in a failure that, used as a hypnotic smokescreen will end up seeming to imply that the existence of another "fact," another "cause," another "reality," a sickly, troublesome and deadly "reality" really exists. It must be remembered and always kept in mind that in the true reality, the harmonious number 4 is always there (like the film in the movie projector analogy previously given) even when a hypnotic smokescreen of mistakes and failures through that distorted lens tries to hide it and state otherwise. In like manner, clouds may temporarily try to hide the reality of the sun but the sun is always there and in fact, is never even aware of "clouds."

In general, instead of the harmonious truth and oneness of reality, the belief of being an imagined, separate, alien ego can only result in the projection of inharmonious lies, illusions, images, and likenesses that are unreal, hypnotic anti-truths. A *separate* ego can only bring forth *separate* untrue meanings of the true meanings and it is always the same conclusion - one simply is the harmonious fact and the other is but a hallucination, a hypnotic illusion that is *still based* on the same harmonious facts and meanings but are *reversed* or misinterpreted to form and project inharmonious and grossly distorted hypnotic dreams. But like all imagined and distorted dreams, they all happily cease upon our awakening.

Real ideas must be established

All ideas, whether correct or mistaken, must originate in mind, the only power capable of producing ideas. Naturally, all good, perfect, and correct ideas originate in Intelligence and imperfect and erroneous ideas originate in mistaken beliefs, a lesson that ceaselessly repeats itself in our daily human lives.[85] We know and understand $2 + 2 = 4$ to be a harmonious fact, checkbooks balance and rockets fly. The fact of our being (just like $2 + 2 = 4$ is an undisputed fact) is that we are all collectively one unity, I AM, an infinite, celestial Life and individual that is impersonal, eternal, harmonious and good, the only cause and the only effect. On the other hand, if we mistakenly believe the erroneous "fact" that 2 + 2 equals anything but 4, inharmonious failures result - checkbooks do not balance and rockets do not fly. Likewise, if we believe ourselves to be finite, distinct and separate egos - erring beliefs of limitations and failures can and do occur in what seems to be, our separate so-called objective, individual lives. The *root and only cause* of the failures that the checkbook did not balance, the rocket did not fly or that limitation, sickness and trouble exists in our so-called objective lives was because *there were erroneous beliefs* in their root creative premises. When the errors, the root causes of all failures were corrected, the failures disappeared. With intelligent reasoning we always went after what we knew to be the root cause, an error, a bad assumption, a false belief or lie in the premise and corrected it. We did not sit there, hope, pray, or somehow mystically treat the unbalanced checkbook that it would mysteriously balance itself, that a rocket would fly or that the limitations and troubles in our lives would go away on their own. In the same way we cannot sit there, hope, pray or somehow mystically treat the failures regarding health, wealth and happiness so that they would miraculously become the desired result by such nonsensical means. We must, armed with intelligent reasoning, always go to the root cause of the error in the premise which is the imagined existence of a separate false ego that hypnotically states otherwise and correct it. We simply cannot believe the resulting hypnotic and inharmonious failure itself is a reality that cannot be changed, as in the case of an unbalanced checkbook, a crashed rocket or limited and troubled, objective lives.

Causes of inharmonious conditions

The root cause of the failures regarding health, wealth and happiness is believing the lie or mistaken belief that we are separated and distinct egos and are not the one infinite Consciousness and cause whose only effect is a universe of harmony, perfection and goodness.[86] Just as an unbalanced checkbook or a crashed rocket will appear automatically when a false belief is utilized in the creative premises, so too will all the resulting or derivative failures appear in our lives when false beliefs about self and our conditions are also held in the premise. Believing to be a so-called separate, alien, wannabe ego will erringly and automatically reflect, that is, cause and throw off a hypnotic awareness of illusions, lies and dreams. It cannot do otherwise; you believe to be separated from the only harmonious Life and so will your life experiences be separated from this harmonious realm as well. In this hypnotic dream, one's being will be separated from the singular, infinite and impersonal perfect celestial Being and will seem to be composed of a separate, finite, material form dependent on so-called material substances in an objective, material universe. This dream progresses on with a rather brief birth-life-death sequence that contains some good but can also contain the undesirable conditions of troubles, loneliness, sicknesses, sufferings, etc., and it always ends in death. Hell of a way to live!

Separate ego usurping the only Ego

In this imaginary dream the consequences of arrogantly attempting to usurp infinite Intelligence, the only cause and Ego there is with a separate cause and ego are dire. The consequences of the arrogant and mistaken claim of being a *separate* ego or consciousness can only be manifested as the *separate,* hypnotic, inharmonious illusions outside of the whole and perfect reality. *Separated* from reality, this hypnotic illusion can only consist of *separate,* numerous, finite, egos, minds, forms, substances and inharmonious qualities that are reversed and distorted lies about the true facts of the one harmonious, celestial Being. Putting it in terms of a cause and effect relationship, the false belief of being a *separate* ego, a *separate,* so-called, thinking, causing ego is the primary error. Attendant to this primary error of a *separate cause* will always be the resultant errors of *separate effects* - that is, illusions of finite forms, objective material substances and less than perfect qualities. These derivative or resultant inharmonious illusions or lies are the direct and inevitable *effects* of the individual belief of being a separate, alien ego that is a *separate cause* and are manifested as so-called objective space containing *separate,* finite forms that seem to be made of so-called matter and inharmoniously existing in a universe of endless birth-life-death cycles.[87]

Correcting the mistakes and failures

In the same way that an unbalanced checkbook can appear to exist but has no staying power over the enlightened mind, so too inharmonious and untrue appearances regarding health, wealth and happiness can appear but have no permanent staying power over the mind that is aware of the truth of what they truly are, what caused them and how they can be terminated or prevented in the first place. We must understand that the most important thing to see is not so much that the inharmonious lie is an illusion-idea hypnotically imagined and therefore can be changed, but to see how outrageous and impossible it is for the cause of this lie to exist at all in the first place! – an imagined, and falsely believed, separate mind and ego that suggests and believes these lies and illusions of its own making - truly unbelievable!

The believed truth of these derivative illusory effects or lies occur simultaneously like clouds hiding the sun or a movie projector lens going out of focus as a result of the main erroneous belief to be a separate ego and cause. It is all governed on a simple cause and effect relationship. On the other hand, these effects, these lies and hypnotic false beliefs cannot be believed to be true if the facts are known both about their illusory nature, their imagined cause and the true state they seem to hide or counterfeit. When one actively entertains this new conviction and awareness of the truth, the true harmonious state and condition will be revealed and found to have always been there and was only temporarily obscured or distorted by a dream brought on by the imagined belief of being outside the perfect, Consciousness of infinite oneness.[88] Remember, as in the theater, you are not making the truth - you are simply letting it Be to enjoy!

All of it, the hypnotic illusion-idea of a physical, objective, universe with separate and multiple material things, beings, egos, minds and causes in it and all the limitation, sickness, war, suffering and death, are nothing more than false effects and beliefs - lies within a dreamlike (or should I say nightmare-like) illusion. All are *individually* derived from the primary error of believing and claiming to be a separate ego and thinking cause outside of and unknown to the only Life, Intelligence, cause and universe there is. As a result of believing to be a separate, alien ego, a separate so-called thinking cause - the resultant, secondary, derivative failures or wrong effects can hypnotically appear on the blackboard, computer output and screen of consciousness incessantly but *only* if this imagined cause and imagined hypnotic effects are believed to be true. When the resultant lies or inharmonious effects are believed to be true by an individual, who is a mistaken believer and now also a victim, another "seeming" reality, another cause other than infinite good is mistakenly believed, experienced and concluded to exist that seems to be separated from and in addition to the only Consciousness or quality there is.[89] Doesn't this aggressive suggestion or lie that an inharmonious reality and cause really exists as a so-called fact, gain admittance in the deluded consciousness every time something goes wrong or a sickness or death occurs and some will say in conceited ignorance, "That is just the way of life." Quite a tenacious war of ideas we have going on here.

Example of bodily pain error

As an example, take the effect of some bodily pain or ache being experienced. The erring, suggestion and belief from the alien mind is that it believes in its ignorance and distorted view that matter or some tissue is a real substance and has cause-ability. Therefore, this tissue is able to conceive, cause, signal, transmit and communicate data to your consciousness. It can independently feel something like the idea of pain (or pleasure if we were looking at an example of bodily pleasure instead of pain - same error). Matter or tissue is never a substance and is merely a shadow in a dream - mental-idea-projection-phenomena subjectively created and residing in consciousness. There is never anything outside of your consciousness. If there were, you would never be able to acknowledge it. It is not an objective thing and has no ability to think, conceive, cause, transmit, or communicate any idea or data whether it is pain, pleasure, distortion, abnormal growth, sickness, exhaustion, cravings, etc. Only mind can formulate these false, unreal beliefs and only the separate alien ego mistakenly believed to be the true "self" can formulate, believe, report and detail the experiences of these imagined failures. Reason through and see the fallacy of this claim that a separate mind is even possible and that this impossible *separate* mind can suggest and believe that matter is a substance and has a separate intelligence to report negative, inharmonious data that is pain (or so-called positive, harmonious data that is pleasure) and affect you. Both are subjective illusions in an imagined mind. There is no *separate* mind other than the one, singular Intelligence and there are certainly no inharmonious *or harmonious* lies or mistakes found in it. Remove your fear or expectations that matter, another mind or anything else has a separate existence, intelligence or cause-ability to direct your fortunes. Life is never a crap shoot or game of chance. It is however, a precise mechanism of effect exactly and minutely reflecting cause in every detail. Therefore, realize your true state that always existed right now, that of the infinite, perfect, Consciousness the only cause and presence, and feel the secure feeling of love, perfection and wholeness that this true awareness will bring, and your health and harmony will be revealed as having never left.

True or false, cause and its effects are one

The only celestial Being in existence, I AM, knows and reveals only its own idea of itself to itself, and this is always infinite, perfect and good and is never finite, discordant, material, or organic illusion-ideas. This awareness, this consciousness of the infinite idea, of the infinite meaning, is the infinite effect, infinite universe, infinite form, Identity, body or *man*ifestation of the one infinite Being, Intelligence, the only cause. The conscious awareness of the idea of itself that is its body and IS the entire universe logically follows life's creative law that effect will always and exactly express its cause. Therefore, the true universe is always a simultaneous and exact reflection of cause within this one Being even if the body of its understanding of self is now infinite and impersonal as well and has transcended so-called finite, material confines. What greater gift and expression of love could infinite Intelligence bestow, than the wakeful awareness of its infinite, perfect, complete, whole and eternal self *individually man*ifested![90]

Because the engine of energetic consciousness is always "awake" or always "running," it always has an active sense and is consciously aware of what it believes, creates, senses, claims or understands itself to be. Right or wrong - it will always automatically cause, throw off, project, manifest and be aware of a "body." This "body," the effect, is always the awareness of a mental universe, a complete *man*ifestation (in consciousness subjectively, of course) that exactly reflects and expresses its sense, belief, understanding or conviction of self whether based on fact or fiction, truth or lies. In other words, mind or cause always automatically throws off, reveals, expresses and becomes aware of its own exact idea and identity of itself subjectively as its manifestation and effect—the reflected and expressed universe within that individual consciousness. Whether they are true ideas or illusion-ideas, either of which, or portions of each, they are always actively caused by the firm beliefs or convictions within, and of, "self." Therefore, Intelligence, the only cause is aware of and is conscious only of itself as one whole, complete, infinite, perfect, idea and the conscious awareness of this idea is its only *man*ifested effect, body or universe. On the other hand, on the imaginary hand, the individual, mistaken belief of being a separate ego automatically causes and reveals the hypnotic awareness of distorted dreams of a finite, material universe containing multiple, inharmonious causes, egos, bodies as in *man,* places and things. In keeping with this false, separate and "many minds" theme, this erroneous "creator" entertains false beliefs that mistakenly assigns multiple intelligences or causes to entities everywhere where they are not - to *separate,* "external" illusion-ideas and *man*ifestations like bodies, substances, drugs, atmospheres, governments, workplaces, inherited proclivities, aging, finances, luck, etc., that the alien mind believes can independently dictate sickness or health, pain or pleasure, chaos or harmony, lack of supply or abundance, etc.

"Go ahead...wreck your day!"

The whole concept of the error that has seemed to have taken place is just as if the one, infinite Ego, Intelligence itself along with its expressed, individual image of itself, the entire universe, had said to arrogant, individual egos that desired to be separate, so-called "thinking" causes of their own devices, "Go ahead...wreck your day! Fall asleep and believe yourselves to be *separate* egos and thinking causes *separated* from your infinite perfect Being which is I AM, the only Life, Ego, thinking cause and universe there is, and in your inevitable hypnotic dreamlike illusions, all the facts and meanings of your harmonious Being and universe will also be *separated*.[91] They will be inharmonious lies turned upside down, out of focus and finitely limited where all the facts and meanings of your life will be distorted and reversed.[92] When you believe yourself to be *separate,* you automatically cease Being You, the all - a whole and perfect universe. The universal creative law of cause and effect dictates that any mind, true or imagined, will always cause and manifest an entire universe as itself. Even for you right now as a human being, that universe that you think you are sitting in, is in fact, YOU! The entire universe you find yourself in will always express your convictions you have of your ENTIRE SELF you believe or understand yourself to be. Therefore, in keeping with this universal creative law, when you believe yourself to be a *separate* mind and being *separated* from your infinite and harmonious Being that is the true universe, you will find yourself a *separate* and finite ego and inharmonious organic being living as a tiny material speck in an immense objective universe. When you believe yourself to be a *separate* life from the only Life you are, you cease knowing true Life that never ends and will now know death and termination that lies and mistakes are very familiar with. Your so-called "life" will now be traveling down a *dead-end* street. When you believe to be *separated* from your harmonious truth, you will know inharmonious illusions, vulnerability and fear. In this imagined nightmare you will be reduced to an incomplete, finite, vulnerable, meat-sack creature with severely limited senses that must toil for the privilege of continuing your aging, inharmonious "life" whose only conclusion is death.[93] Once you tire of that *separate illusion,* and *you will,* I will always be ready with open arms to receive your reawakening self back to the only reality and once again reveal yourself *as,* I AM ALL and I AM ONE; the only perfect Life, Being and universe there is."[94]

Left unchecked, the ignorant and childish alien mind has absolutely no knowledge, respect nor understanding of the one, perfect Intelligence or one harmonious cause and Ego. In aggressive, mindless malice it runs riot in the mistaken belief of "minds many" seemingly generating and revealing multiple, *separate,* inharmonious causes everywhere where they are not. All this is occurring within the big bang objective universe struggling in seemingly endless limitations and birth-life-death cycles that is all an illusion unbeknownst to the mistaken believer and victim. Throughout it all, true or false, your entire life experience and universe which is really the full manifestation of you and *is you,* is *man*ifesting itself subjectively within *individual* consciousness, the *only entity* life will find itself in.

Big bang universe invalid

In this line of reasoning it is noted that the objective, physical universe has been very aptly named the big bang. That it is but nothing more than that. Just a bang and, in fact, a very weak, impotent bang *separated* from reality. Just a minor, little bang for it was nothing more than a counterfeit, imagined, hypnotic, illusion-bang from an erring, immature, malevolent child's cap gun. A mere secondary effect-smoke-screen of manifested lies and false beliefs on the movie screen of subjective consciousness behind which the primary or inciting error hides that caused it—the belief and claim of a *separate,* alien so-called thinking cause and ego. A liar claiming to be a thinking cause outside of, in addition to, or even to the exclusion of the Great Blast of Truth that is I AM, the only Intelligence, the only thinking cause, the only Soul, Life, Being, individual, body, universe or conscious awareness there ever was or ever will be. The erroneous illusion-idea and hypnotic dreams of an objective, material universe composed of finite, separate, physical things, beings, egos and inharmonious causes everywhere, is a hypnotic lie from the start and has been shown to possess no real basis in intelligent reasoning. Nothing but an out of focus lens on our Life projector. The phenomena of the seemingly physical, objective universe known as the big bang are nothing but the resultant, derivative effects stemming from the false claim and *individual belief* of being *a separate, alien ego and cause.* This imagined and impossible alien mind and its automatically resultant lies, illusions and hypnotic dreams and effects are nothing but cheap, counterfeit, imitations. Believed, they are hypnotic, aggressive, harmful, inharmonious beliefs and effects contrary to the real celestial Deal that is I AM, the only true individual, Being, cause, effect and universe in existence. In this one and only Great Blast of Truth that is me and my universal body - the ONLY CAUSE AND THE ONLY EFFECT - I AM not even aware of, nor have I caused the effect of a silly objective big bang universe illusion or any other false illusions-ideas, opposing lies or imagined, hypnotic dreams.[95] And I Am *certainly not aware* of an unreal, imagined, *separate, alien* mind that has supposed and dreamed up these illusions of an objective big bangy universe. These lies and imagined effects are all out of focus, counterfeit, wrong, limited, inverted and opposing interpretations and meanings of me and my infinite attributes of my manifested universe and are *always* the result of the erroneous belief of being a *separate,* alien ego, a *separate* cause outside of, and unknown to me. The *separate* ego derived illusory universe is a sad joke at best suggesting and revealing lies and anti-truths of I AM in what seems to be, an idiotic quest for an imagined life and creator to be mistakenly acknowledged as a real cause of a finite, physical reality. The action of mind can never escape the active and universal creative law of cause and effect, that in this case, is a pathetic wannabe mind and its counterfeit so-called material man in a counterfeit so-called material universe![96]

Opposing lies reversed point to the facts

On the other hand, on the positive, constructive hand all meanings of opposing illusions of form, substance and quality of the inharmonious, so-called objective universe indicate when reversed, to be the true, eternal and harmonious facts within the only universe there is - I AM ALL. Therefore, when we erroneously believed in the hypnotic illusion-idea of death, it was found to be the silly lie, illusion and failure about the idea and fact that I AM one, infinite, continuous, eternal Life. When we erroneously believed in the hypnotic illusion-idea that there are separate, multiple, inharmonious minds, egos and causes, it was found to be the mindless lie and illusion about the idea and fact that I AM ONE. I AM THE ONLY INDIVIDUAL THAT IS A HARMONIOUS UNITY. I AM THE ONLY EGO AND THE ONLY CAUSE. When we erroneously believed in the hypnotic illusion-idea of physical space containing planets, stars and other phenomena made of numerous material substances, it was all found to be the idiotic lie and illusion about the idea and fact that I understand that I AM the only universe and that I AM made of the substance of my ideas, always infinite, perfect and good. When we hypnotically believed in being multiple, finite, sentient, sexual, material bodies having separate being and intelligence capable of pleasure or pain, health or sickness, lack or abundance and living in a so-called objective universe, it was found to be the malicious lie and illusion about the idea and fact that my body is the only universe there is which consists entirely of my awareness and understanding of myself in this perfect impersonal Consciousness - I AM person-less, infinite, whole and complete Intelligence containing and individually conscious of all the abundant good there ever was or ever will be.[97] When we erroneously believed in the hypnotic illusion-idea of imperfection, it was found to be the reckless lie, illusion and distorted meaning about the idea and fact that I AM perfection. When we erroneously believed that we must eat dead plants and animals to sustain life, it was found to be the barren lie and distorted meaning about the idea and fact that I AM the only truth and Life that is the *only food* necessary for Life.[98] When we erroneously believed in personal sicknesses, it was found to be the unhealthy lie, illusion and distorted meaning about the idea and fact that I AM impersonal and therefore always know perfect health that is painless and harmonious. When we erroneously believed in aging and time, it was found to be the worn out lie, illusion and distorted meaning about the idea and fact that I AM *now,* forever perfect and timeless like 2 + 2 = 4. When we erroneously believed in any limitation or inharmonious idea within the false objective universe, it was found to be the illusion and distorted meaning about the idea and fact that I AM the only universe, the only Consciousness, the only infinity and reality and I AM always harmonious.

Stated once more for good measure, lies, failures, distorted meanings and inharmonious illusions are always the resultant, false, hypnotic belief-effects of the primary error, the main, root error and this main, root error is individually believing and claiming to be a *separate,* alien ego, a *separate,* so-called intelligence and thinking cause, a liar whose very existence, awareness, substance and life is a hypnotic illusion. As with all wrong concepts, a liar and its lies are imagined and false and will always "die" or cease to be and in so doing, reveal the truth. Reverse and destroy any of these hypnotic lies, illusions, and distorted meanings and you will have the truth—the truth that has always been there—the true state of the one, eternal, harmonious Life and reality. One harmonious cause reflected and expressed as one harmonious effect, as one harmonious Being - the true universe. By specifically reversing any lie, in essence you are translating the distorted language and meaning of an untrue lie into the language and meaning of the true fact it is hiding and distorting. Although it is true and is a fact that 2 + 2 = 4, it is of absolutely no use when confronted with the illusion of 27 x 2 = 89. Only the pertinent and specific solution and fact that 27 x 2 = 54 need be applied to reverse and correct the inharmonious illusion at hand.

I AM the only reality, the only cause, the only Being, the only Soul, the only Consciousness, the only truth, the only love and the only Life and Identity there ever has been or ever will be. I know myself as the only perfect, whole and complete universe or body there is. I AM simply everywhere and my perfect "AM" can be revealed everywhere *including* anywhere and anytime within the illusion of the big bang universe as simply as correcting the mistake of 27 x 2 = 89 with 27 x 2 = 54 works no matter where you happen to be. The true facts of eternal life, perfect harmony, health, abundance and happiness are available everywhere always - they just need to be revealed and actively known.[99] The hypnotic illusions and effects revealed as an objective, inharmonious, material big bang universe never presented factual evidence of any reality but were malevolent trespassers of the truth. Mere resultant counterfeits and opposing lies, dreams, shadows, illusions, failures and distorted meanings about the true facts, the true effects about I AM and my perfect, harmonious attributes and universe. In the same way that a shadow can only present a limited and distorted image or meaning of the true object or idea casting the shadow, so too the big bang universe can only present a finite, faint and distorted image and meaning of the true universe and Identity that is ME - I AM. The illusion-effect of a big bang physical universe and every objective "thingy" in it only serves to provide a secondary, illusory smokescreen to hide the primary, root origin and cause of these opposing lies, effects and phenomena - the imaginary, individual and hypnotic belief in being a *separate,* alien ego—a *separate,* so-called thinking cause and liar—that for us, began with our own *separate,* individual, *human* conception, birth, and identity.[100]

Chapter 5

Identity Theft!

Inharmonious ideas and false effects are illusions but need a mistaken believer to believe in them in order for these illusions to "live," to be "real," known and acknowledged as "truth." Logically, all ideas, effects, and illusions, true or false, require a similarly true or false consciousness to generate and acknowledge them as a "fact" respectively. The true or false nature of an idea, the effect, is always directly linked to its respective true or false consciousness, the only cause that could create it. True ideas or false illusions that are revealed on that movie screen of conscious awareness, do not mysteriously come from nowhere or randomly by chance as human beliefs would have it - logically they must have a germane source that caused them to appear. Effects exactly reflect their cause. Therefore, in this revealing process, pedigree is always maintained just as Intelligence does not generate false, inharmonious illusion-ideas, so too whacked-out ignorance does not generate true, harmonious ideas. If it did it would no longer be ignoring the facts thereby remaining ignorant. In other words, false beliefs or lies, to have any effect, need a liar to conceive and voice them *and* a believer to believe in them. Due to the infinite nature of Intelligence and its corresponding infinite quantity of facts and effects it caused, it has been reasoned that every erroneous, inharmonious idea or effect *must be,* and can *only be* a lie, a mistaken belief in a distorted idea *about an already established* intelligent, harmonious fact.

Of course, without the solid rock of reasoning and understanding to support its position, a mere belief in a true idea, even though correct, cannot be trusted in times of stress questioning its validity. Like all baseless and unsupported beliefs, this position will be like building on sand. Even if correct, it is still merely a belief and not a firm, *understood* fact. When stress and doubt question its position and integrity, the belief, not being supported by the rock of intelligent reasoning and understanding why some harmonious fact is a fact, can change to some other position and will eventually drop down to its native, shifting sands of doubt and confusion.

Separate, alien ego needs mistaken believers to seemingly "be"

Due to the oneness or infinite nature of Intelligence that is the only Ego and reality, an erroneous belief can have only one source and that is a separate, alien ego and mind who is a liar whose existence itself, is a lie about the "oneness" of infinite Intelligence - the only Being there is in reality. Because of this direct link between the nature of ideas and the respective consciousness that generated and believes in them, an individual entertaining only intelligent, harmonious facts about an issue excludes all lies and false beliefs regarding that particular issue. This active knowing and entertaining the true facts simultaneously denies the separate, alien ego "life" or "being" in that consciousness on that issue. This seemingly insidious, separate ego needs beliefs in its lies to "be," to seemingly exist or to have life, because that is what its existence is based or supported upon - erring beliefs. In the exact proportion that its numerous lies are believed to be true, in that exact proportion does a separate ego seem to be, exist and have life. The soul of the alien ego then seems to simultaneously replace the soul or identity of you regarding the erring beliefs in question. I say "seem to" because lies and their creator do not really exist as a reality but only as a false illusion.

Identity theft

A mistaken believer can never really be you because as has been shown through reasoning, you are the one and only true Ego that is always consciously and accurately aware of this truth, of this fact of your infinite, eternal Life and self; perfection and oneness everywhere. This accurate awareness of the individual self as perfection and oneness everywhere, as all ideas and effects, is the only "offspring" of

Intelligence, the only manifested phenomena in existence.[101] Similarly, the mistaken believer as an imagined alien ego always causes and is aware of false ideas, effects, lies and illusions. They are all mistakenly believed to be true thereby framing an inharmonious existence of untold millions of separated individuals suffering in their seemingly endless birth-life-death dreams. This active and firm conviction of being separate from the one, perfect, infinite Mind and Life in a so-called material universe of multiple, discordant minds and bodies is the only "offspring" or "sons and daughters" of non-intelligence and ignorance that can temporarily occupy the position of your true Ego. It does this in the exact ratio that the subject, erring, *separate* ego and its suggested lies are believed to be true.[102] Lies, false ideas and illusions generated by a mistaken believer (mistaken believer being the same as a separate ego) are all outside of and unknown to *infinite* Intelligence that is your true Identity, your true Ego, your true Self. Lies and erring beliefs, like the example of bodily pain previously given of the fallacy of supposed separate, intelligent matter reporting various sensory data, cannot exist safely or permanently within a consciousness that is becoming enlightened as to its true nature through sound, intelligent reasoning. Hypnotic lies and believed inharmonious effects can only reside within an individual when the individual is temporarily blinded to the facts of infinite harmony and truth everywhere because of fear, carelessness, ignorance or past erring cultural and personal beliefs self-generated or handed down. In all cases of this blindness, the individual is just going along on flimsy, false beliefs and has performed insufficient reasoning to see their false, erroneous nature. In the ignorant and mistaken state of believing to be a separate ego, we erroneously believe the illusion of matter (among many other false beliefs) to be an actual substance possessing being and intelligence and therefore, cause. Our mistaken sense of self as being a separate ego somehow integrated within an actual material body with its own cause-ability was never a fact, but it did appear this way, but only as a hypnotic illusion produced by the believer that now seemed to be yourself.[103] Herein lies the mechanism, occurrence, and scope of this insidious identity theft. Through mistakenly believing lies and erroneous, inharmonious ideas to be facts, you, your true, intelligent self that was consciously aware of your one and only perfect, harmonious, celestial Ego and universe is temporarily stolen or lost sight of. A false sense, a false conviction of "you" is now believed to be your true "self" as this liar, this imagined ego aggressively steals its place as your "self," life and identity.[104] As was shown, consciousness, without the rudder of intelligent reasoning, is like a blackboard or movie screen where any idea or effect can appear whether true fact or distorted, hypnotic illusions including your own perceived identity depending on your conclusions and convictions what you believe about self to be true.

As has also been reasoned previously, who can state with a conviction, with a firm belief, that the mental effect of matter is a substance that possesses intelligence to independently cause sickness or health, but a blind, unreasoning believer that can only be an imagined, separate, alien ego outside of, and unknown to the only Ego there is? Who can state with a conviction that the effect of space is a real physical volume but an erroneous believer that again, was shown to be an imagined, separate, alien ego? In reality who are you - the blind and duped believer and victim believing in lies and dreams, or are you the one intelligent Mind who does not cause, harbor nor give reality to reversals of the truth that are presented as lies, false illusions and hypnotic dreams? Clearly YOU ARE, as revealed through sound reasoning, the *individual* conscious awareness of the true Self; the one Intelligence, the one Entity, the only Soul, the only cause and Being of infinite perfection that is fully awake and never dreaming. Therefore, whenever we find ourselves entertaining any illusion as a fact, we are inadvertently submitting, in a proportional measure, to identity theft by diminishing the awareness of our complete, true, Intelligent Ego, our true, singular, harmonious Life. In the same measure that we do this, we are granting a separate, alien ego "life" and must now live and be victimized with the inharmonious consequences these very erroneous beliefs cause in its illusory "life" or hypnotic dream. It is only through this identity theft of the individual Ego that the erring belief of a separate ego can seem to live or have being as you, a finite material being in a material universe and be victimized by the resultant inharmonious consequences of its lies, false beliefs and imagined, hypnotic dreams that threaten your health, wealth, and happiness.

Alien ego a parasite

In this respect, the imagined, separate ego has the nature of a parasite because it cannot live or have being without imposing itself on a host ego by way of identity theft. Without the identity theft of the host ego, the lies and false arguments are simply unexpressed and unknown. This theft of one's true Identity can only occur when we are not actively entertaining the truth and facts of our true Identity as the one, infinite, perfect, eternal Life that is aware of itself as a complete, perfect, infinite

Being or presence everywhere. Inadvertently or carelessly we succumb into believing self to be a separate, extraneous ego, and like all ego and mentality, is always an active cause of its individual universe. This erring distorted cause can only bring forth reversals of the facts with lies that are always inharmonious, finite and hypnotic illusion-ideas. More succinctly, the separated ego unfortunately believes itself to be a mind locked into a finite material body that is but a minute speck in an immense material universe with all its negative, limiting challenges that then terminates in death for all. On the other hand, the real self right now understands itself to be the only presence and universe there is, whereas the organic man and its material universe existed only as a temporary hypnotic illusion. Vainly it seeks to hide the true universe of self that is oneness and perfection. As it has been reasoned, illusion-ideas are specific lies and reversals about an infinite quantity of specific, harmonious ideas and effects and therefore, in reversing these real harmonious ideas, must be inharmonious illusions possessing no reality.

Soldiers of deceit

When we believe to be a separate, alien ego, this mistaken ego is certainly not without its soldiers of deceit that seem to testify against and obscure the true Identity of you and the oneness of your Being. These soldiers of deceit are the five finite and limited organs where the various sense perceptions are believed to reside within the so-called, physical body. Relentlessly they seem to pour forth their false evidence and lies to convince you that the resultant illusion-idea of the physical, objective universe and physical bodies including yours is the real deal and this is where your supposed, finite, material life tenaciously resides. Eyes seem to testify that it all certainly looks to be a material universe, ears seem to concur that it certainly sounds like a material universe along with the nose that it smells like one, the mouth that it tastes like one and the whole body in general that it certainly feels like one. Where do these organs get their ability to testify to anything including this dream of a material universe made of substantial, objective illusion-ideas? Again, with our clear reasoning we have seen that the so-called physical body and the organs composing it must simply be mental phenomena or effects held *subjectively* in mind as illusion-ideas and can never have substance or cause-ability themselves that is always required for testimony or data input and output of any kind. Just as the hypnotic illusion that consciousness occurs within the mental idea-effect of a brain that was earlier shown to be a myth, so too ideas such as eyes, ears, nose, etc., are mere mental idea-effects and cannot intelligently initiate or create other ideas or sensing activities like seeing, hearing, smelling, etc., of their own accord. This illusion is clearly illustrated in that a hypnotized individual can have sense testimony manipulated to be different from everyone else nearby. Clearly it is not the so-called organs of sense that are doing the sensing when the hypnotized individual bears testimony contrary to those around him. Only consciousness can contain the activity of the senses and our senses were never dependent on the illusion-ideas of brains, eyes, ears, nose, etc., to input or output data. However, understanding that the senses are not dependent on physical organs is uncovering this illusion only partially. It must also be understood that the actual sensory details of a finite, material, objective reality is also erroneous and is the mistaken, hypnotic evidence of a realm that simply does not exist. Impersonal mind is the only medium in existence and on this blackboard or movie screen of universal consciousness, unreal, erroneous ideas, lies and illusions can and do appear and in this case, as the so-called physical organs of the five senses residing in and providing data about an imaginary, finite, material, objective realm.

Ignorantly and blindly succumbing to believing self to be a separate ego automatically results in reversals and lies of every true, harmonious idea, creating illusions of limited, finite, objective, material "reality" with all its multiple, inharmonious "intelligent" causes to challenge you. The malevolent separated ego extends its vulnerable, suffering, imaginary being as you, the victim, for yet another day. That imaginary being or life is certainly not a glorious one, for its "life" sadly consists of all the vulnerability, sickness, disease, suffering, poverty, confusion, chaos, fear and death of the human experience. The so-called life that is the hypnotic dream of this death oriented ego will not cease until we waken, increase our understanding of the facts and deny this Impostor "life" by ceasing to blindly believe in being a separate ego along with all its malicious and harmful lies and illusions. This can only be accomplished by the individual through intelligent reasoning and understanding what is truly going on in his or her life.

Human ego the highest manifestation of the alien ego

Person or personal is only an illusion of mental phenomena, of finite ideas occurring within impersonal, invisible consciousness. Just like the one and only factual Ego is an impersonal entity, so too the imagined, separate, alien ego can only be an impersonal entity.[105] No entity exists other than impersonal consciousness, the realm that envelops all phenomena, real facts or false illusions. The highest manifestation or erring idea of this impersonal alien ego is the human ego, the belief of a distinct human consciousness; a mind believed to be separated from the one, infinite and complete Being.[106] One's erroneous belief and conviction in being a separate ego is identical to the erring belief of a human being, the belief of a separated, organic, human mind, ego, body and life. In whatever negative way that the aggressive, false, insidious, deadly, alien ego and liar can be described with all its resultant vulnerability, misery, confusion, violence, fear, death and so forth in victimizing you, so too the imposing human ego can be described, as they are one and the same; imagined, arrogant and deadly.[107] It must be exposed as the imagined, nightmarish impostor and liar it truly is. Henceforth, I will use the terms, separate, alien ego and the human ego interchangeably when discussing its fullest erring manifestation - the human being.

We are the only power that can make this false ego and its lies real by believing that it and its lies are real. This imagined human ego and the resultant lies, false ideas, and effects suggested by this false creator gain admittance by two methods. These are when we allow it knowingly or inadvertently into our convictions about self. A separate, alien ego does not care whether the resultant, erroneous beliefs be of fear; of bodily, sensual pleasure, sickness, disease or pain; of mind or cause in matter as in a thinking brain contained within a sentient body; of unhappiness, depression, loneliness, hate, ill will, dishonesty, destructive criticism, jealousy, hurt feelings and incompleteness; of an objective universe made of material substances with their inherent inharmonious causes that is mind in matter; of life that needs to be born in order to live; of life that lives in and is dependent on matter or that $2 + 2 = 5$, 3 or 7, etc., etc., as long as it is an inharmonious lie, a reversal of the truth and is believed to be true. When these illusions are believed to be true, it is there where you become the victim of them. Also, many of these mistaken beliefs within yourself may now be applied to individuals other than yourself as in the instances where the imagined, mistaken belief conjures up the situation and appearance that someone else holds ill will, jealousy or hate towards you or they possess other negative attributes and qualities. In the oneness of infinite Intelligence and Being, even the belief of "others" having separate, individual minds is an illusion. Furthermore, to believe that these separate, individual minds can think wrongly, hold ill will or other negative qualities are still more mistaken, hypnotic illusions. These erroneous beliefs applied to "others" as separate, "intelligent" thinking causes that can be inharmonious and undesirable are equally destructive in destroying your harmony because you are the only one there! There is not one legitimate false and inharmonious belief even if it *seems to be* outside of self and *seems to be* about "others" including other places and other things. False beliefs believed to be true, will automatically grant and cause inharmonious failures and negative experiences with you as the victim. It will grant more life to a false, miserable separate ego who replaces your true Identity in proportion to the errors you believe to be true. Any lie or erroneous belief occurring within the illusion-idea of an objective universe that is believed to be true supports the imagined existence and validity of an imaginary, separate, alien ego. Simultaneously, its life or ego seems to aggressively displace your true Ego and Life in this insidious, invisible mechanism of identity theft that humans "enjoy."

Basis of forgiveness

Within the infinite oneness of universal Consciousness, intelligent, true Being correctly understands all and never needs to believe anything, true or false. It knows and understands all because it is all and all is within itself, harmonious Intelligence. Infinite Intelligence never made a mistake but when this one Ego is temporarily hidden by the false belief of being a separate ego, that in our case is the human ego, and some error or mistake is *inevitably* made, we blindly and erroneously believe that it was our self who made the mistake. After all, up to that time it was the only "self" and identity we knew of.[108] Our true Identity, the one Intelligence and only reality there is cannot make mistakes just like mathematics cannot make mistakes. Only a misunderstanding, a mistaken belief outside of and unknown to the one Intelligence can make mistakes. When we, identifying and believing ourselves to be human beings, make a mistake and not realizing that the mind that made this mistake is the false one installed through identity theft, we unwittingly condemn ourselves as if we, our true self and identity in fact, made the mistake.[109] Up to this point, this imagined human self is the only self and identity we were aware of. Also one does not have to look very far for "other" imagined, separate human egos who may wholeheartedly and maliciously agree, albeit ignorantly, with your self-condemnation. This indicates the depth, scope and silent, invisible, subtlety of the illusion and operation of the theft of your true Identity. Now there is a battle where the idiot, separate, human ego frequently and easily wins almost every time in its own self-inflicted victimization! What a victory for the idiot, separate, alien, human ego when not only are we unaware of our true self and that identity theft has already taken place for a mistake to be made at all, but we then go on and agree with this lying impostor that it is us, the only "self" we knew of at that time, who made the mistake and condemn ourselves accordingly.

Even we, as human beings recognize the inherent goodness within our own heart that is in fact, our true Ego and Identity and even though we do not understand the real cause of the mistake, we still intuitively struggle to reject the insidious and subtle nature of identity theft that has caused harm to ourselves and others. Isn't this rejection of the false ego that, for a time seems to be our only ego, is what's really taking place when we make a mistake, see the error, experience a change of heart, and ask forgiveness from ourselves and others whom we may have offended? Although we may not be aware of it, that change of heart is really, in a measure, the rejection of our false ego and the regaining of our true Ego of Good by forgiving ourselves and asking others for forgiveness, if applicable.

Being familiar with the insidious nature of identity theft allows us to more easily forgive ourselves. Also, understanding the insidious nature of identity theft enlarges our ability to forgive others when it is clear, that in their contrite hearts, they too are seeking to reject that false, malevolent ego and are struggling to realign themselves closer once more to the one, true, harmonious Identity. Of course if you are unwilling to forgive others, you will have a hard time forgiving yourself and finding peace in your own heart when that time comes because your own mind can never be a hypocrite to itself because in truth, there exists only one, singular Mind.[110]

Inherent stumbling blocks

You, the only Intelligence and Ego, are incapable of making errors or mistakes. It is only when we are so overcome with the resultant lies presented as the illusion-identity of a human being struggling within, fearing and lusting over the illusion-ideas of persons, places and things in the so-called physical world that seems to contain the illusion of a real past, present and future, that we so tragically believe an almost infinite number of unimaginable stumbling blocks to prevent us from knowing our true Identity, the one, perfect, Ego and Life.[111] This does not have to remain this way any longer. We have the ability through our intelligent reasoning to work our way up and out of the mistake of believing to be separate egos that is causing all the vulnerability, fear, limitations, erroneous desires, sufferings, and tragedies of these erroneous human beliefs and illusions. These erroneous human beliefs and illusions were never facts or reality but were all simply worthless, imagined lies about the truth, the *one* perfect and harmonious truth.

Assertion of the truth through reason

You, the impersonal, infinite, one and only Being, are absolutely complete, perfect, and good because that is the only condition that Intelligence, the only reality, the only thinking cause can find its awareness of itself to be. You may ask, what is going on when I do not actively know, feel, sense or realize the truth of oneness, perfection and good that is so prevalent in the impeded human experience? Any inharmonious sense of separateness, imperfection, sickness, fear, confusion, materiality, finiteness, incompleteness, limitation, lack, etc. (which are untrue lies and illusions), always occur as a result of the same root cause - identity theft - in believing to be a separate, alien ego, a separate thinking mind. This separated mind aggressively conjures up, suggests, argues, and hypnotically projects the illusion and lie about the true Identity of self along with all those other separate inharmonious causes and illusions that you may or may not believe depending on your knowledge and understanding of the facts of Being. However, you now know and understand fact from fiction in this arena. You, in allowing identity theft to take place knowingly or inadvertently, can suffer through these lies and false effects by believing them and their causes to be fact, or you can now aggressively assert your true Identity as the one, infinite, perfect Being that is the ONLY MENTAL CAUSE AND PRINCIPLE OF PERFECT EFFECTS through careful, intelligent reasoning and thereby reverse and destroy these silly, mistaken beliefs about inharmonious causes and effects that aggressively seek to delude and harm you. In so doing you will reject and reverse all the opposing lies about the truth and assert the true, harmonious facts and meanings of health, abundance and happiness in their place. In so doing you gain release from the negative illusion-ideas and their causes, and in the same proportion, gain release from the dreamlike, hypnotic belief and illusion of being an imagined, ignorant alien ego separated from the one infinite impersonal Ego. This erring belief of a separate ego is, of course, the human ego - ignorant, arrogant, personal, selfish, suspicious, full of doubt, harmful, and deadly. Any false and inharmonious sense of lack of perfect ease (dis-ease) found in self or observed in others such as sickness, disease, fear, hate, lust, greed, jealousy, criticism, intelligent matter possessing cause-ability, unhappiness, crime, depression, imperfection, limitation, etc., etc., can be sourced back to the same root cause of all lies and false effects, the belief in being *another* thinking mind; a *separate* ego, the lying human ego that is ignorant, selfish, harmful and deadly to itself.

Your true Identity is the impersonal, infinite and perfect Mind and there is no other Life, Individual, Consciousness, thinking Cause, Identity, or Soul. You are untouchable by any erroneous idea to the contrary that seeks to victimize you because in actively knowing, feeling, sensing and realizing what the true idea is - your true Identity that is impersonal Life, infinite perfection and good residing everywhere, it is impossible at the same time to believe in and fear the lies, threats and nightmares of the make-believe separated, finite, malevolent human mind and all its imagined, objective causes and ill-effects.[112] *Just relax and let it Be* - the harmonious truth of one infinite Being was always there and cannot be lost nor disappear!

False concepts need your fear and false beliefs to appear real

Will you inherit or develop some disease? Will you find yourself in short supply of anything? Will you catch a cold because of wet feet or contagion? Will you end up with any of the endless parade of painful illnesses and limitations that print media, television and radio suggests you will get if you don't discuss and utilize some new so-called material-substance drug with your doctor? Will wars and strife throughout the world spiral into uncontrollable chaos? Will local, national or world economies affect you negatively or positively without your control? Will your loneliness, incompleteness and unhappiness ever end? Will indulging in drugs or alcohol to feel good or mask pain really work when the only good to feel is the awareness of the facts and truth of your real nature? How can addictions to various substances occur when we know there is no substance or power out there that is out of our control? The list of resultant lies, illusions and their imagined causes just goes on and on in these nightmares but not in the sense that it can wear you down as if they were something real that needs to be dealt with. When the truth is found, that is, understood and known, the false belief in a lie about this truth and its counterfeit source no matter how aggressive, is always acknowledged as unreal and is never feared, but is simply reversed, overruled, dismissed and forgotten.

Face and reverse illusions and fear armed with the Truth

Let the malicious human ego relentlessly present lying arguments and subtle suggestions. In a seeming effort to gain presence, life and "reality" in your true Soul, false sensory testimony about numerous causes, ill-effects and illusions appear. But now in your peaceful and fearless ease of a greater understanding, you now know how hypnotic illusions and their only source appeared, but most importantly, you now know, feel and realize the wonderful, loving and perfect reality that is the Truth.[113] As has been shown, all beliefs, lies, and false illusions are simply specific and opposing reversals of true, harmonious ideas, that by implication seem to be silently suggesting and arguing for another reality to victimize you when believed. All illusions can only be nurtured by your fear of them being real through not understanding the truth about them, and all are an imagined nightmare stuffed with fear, lack, unhappiness, misery, and death. Therefore, when the inharmonious and hypnotic lies and illusions of sickness, depression, unhappiness, loneliness, incompleteness, criticism, intelligent matter, substance abuse, overindulgence, lack of money, aging, loss of vitality, etc, etc., either as being present or as a future possibility, are suggested and believed within what seems to be your own mind and life, a negative feeling of *fear* is conjured up as if they had real external causes.[114] Immediately and forcefully know that they are simply false reversals of the true state and are nothing but a lying dreamlike argument from the alien imposing ego and there is nothing to fear.[115] Actively reason, know and feel that you - I AM is pure Intelligence, the only thinking cause that has only one effect and this can only be the harmonious and perfect, conscious awareness of I AM everywhere.[116] Only health, abundance, harmony, completion, happiness, and perfection can be found in the awareness of your true Identity. "I AM ONE, THE ONLY MENTAL CAUSE AND MY IDEA OF MYSELF IS THE ONLY EFFECT, THE ONLY ETERNAL UNIVERSE, THE ONLY *MANIFESTATION* WHOSE *IMAGE AND LIKENESS* IS ALWAYS PERFECT."

Again, no one else can do this work and realization for you. As the whole universe, I AM has always been the manifestation and awareness of the only Life, Intelligence and Being there is along with all the abundance, peace and harmony inherent to this singular and infinite Being.[117] Your only effort is not to battle and fight lies and illusions as if there was something real there to struggle with, mistakenly implying their true existence and real cause, which *fear* clings to. Rather, specifically reverse the opposing lies and false hypnotic illusions, reinstate the truth and continuously know and *fearlessly* feel the truth and perfection of your true, impersonal, celestial Being as the only Life, presence, and creator there is harmoniously encompassing all.[118] There is no *real* separate creator of discord and lack of harmony and therefore there is no *real* creator to fear or destroy, only the *belief* that *another* creator can exist must be destroyed - the *imagined* separate alien ego. You correct the error of believing and fearing an illusion and lie by realizing the comforting and relaxing truth about it.[119] You reverse the illusory lie, the false belief whether it be a separate ego, sickness, lack, trouble, death, etc., and reveal the fact and true state about I AM which the lie was attempting to hide in its seeming efforts to victimize you.[120] See the truth through these hypnotic illusions and lies by reversing them and thereby the truth and true conditions of I AM will be revealed.

True conditions were always manifested and were always the true facts and can again be revealed and uncovered by destroying the false beliefs and fears that obscure them. Seeking to cast off and end the horrors of a hypnotic nightmare, as if the material universe and the material "you" were real things to be cast off, will never end the ordeal. You never destroy the horror of a nightmare by thinking it is real and then wishing this "something real" were gone. These are contradictions that will never unravel. You cease the horror of a nightmare by waking up and realizing the fact that it was nothing but a bad dream, a hypnotic illusion at best. Contemplate the perfect, harmonious, wakened, reality of impersonal, perfect Consciousness, the only subjective thinking cause and presence and do not fear an imagined, false, chaotic, human ego and its untrue ill-effects as real.[121]

I know it may not be the easiest thing to do at first, but we must change our habits of thought that actively believed in and feared these hypnotic illusions all our lives. We must form new *fearless points of view* through intelligent reasoning what is real and what are mere illusions through actively knowing the truth. We must change the model we are focused upon and actively and aggressively become aware, know and realize that a harmonious and secure REALITY of OUR ONE PERFECT BEING is our ONLY model instead of the imagined, separate human ego's finite, material and deathly model. In time and through practice it will become easier and in doing so, we are engaging in the final war for the awareness of our true Identity that will be eternally revealed through this means.

Your thoughts and feelings today create your experiences tomorrow

Individual conscious awareness or life itself is the infinite blackboard, computer or movie screen that will dutifully express whatever we choose to experience through our thoughts and feelings. Our thoughts and feelings regarding self are our convictions about what is true and what is not true about the identity and condition of self. As a reminder, it was noted that the so-called thinking ability of a believed-to-be-separate mind is not really thinking at all, but can only be mistaken distortions of all true harmonious facts turned upside down. The individual's thoughts and feelings that are convictions about self, are the only input to that infinite blackboard, computer or movie screen of manifested experience. It will then express and become aware of exactly the precise nature and identity of the "self" that has been *individually* put there previously. This process of conscious, self-identity with conviction, that is, with strong thoughts and feelings about what is real, about what is true is the only creative activity in consciousness and is the only creative mechanism there is. It is the only mechanism of creation there ever was. In short, thoughts and feelings you entertain today about the nature and identity of you, of your self, will manifest and be exactly what you will experience shortly thereafter. Our convictions today dictate the quality or lack of quality of our lives tomorrow. Like computers, good data in will create a good result out and to be sure, garbage in will always result in garbage out with the certainty of clock-work-like accuracy. The experiences in our lives were never the result of luck, chance, being in the right place at the right time, etc., etc., or all the other fantasy causes or blame we may find acceptable in our culture. The universal law of creativity dictates that thoughts and feelings *individually* held in one's heart, that is, in your convictions of what is believed or understood to be true about the identity of you, your universe and all the ideas in it, is the only creator there is. Eventually we all must take responsibility for our individual lives and make adjustments in our convictions and life experiences accordingly.

Mechanism that manifests experiences as its offspring

The mistaken belief of self being a *separate,* human ego with its so-called independent thinking ability will always result in *separate,* negative suggestions of lies and erroneous convictions that are all anti-truths, that when believed to be true, simultaneously generate a feeling of *fear* that they are real and true. After all, a nightmare could not be a frightful nightmare unless we knew the details of it first and then felt and believed (feared) these details to be true - in short, a negative conviction. When both the "knowing" of the erring idea and the "feeling," that is, the fear of it being real are present forming the negative conviction or belief, they will, with certainty, always cause and manifest the negative experience—the hypnotic nightmare for you, the deluded and victimized human ego. You are now free to turn it around and reveal the good and positive condition and experience that was always there with the very same principle that was utilized in manifesting the negative experience. Both the knowing and feeling elements combined constitute conviction or solid belief, and both are necessary to manifest anything, good or bad, reality or illusion. So when your human ego confronts you with a negative suggestion, argument or erring enticement, (all mistaken beliefs outside reality) turn them around, that is, reverse them to their harmonious opposite while simultaneously knowing the truth through sound reasoning that YOU ARE the *individual* conscious awareness of the infinite Ego, the perfect, impersonal Being, THE ONLY THINKING CAUSE AND ITS PERFECT IDEA OF ITSELF - THE ONLY EFFECT - THE ONLY UNIVERSE THAT IS I AM. You are not the individual conscious awareness of the fearful, lustful, lying, idiot separate ego and its whacked-out illusion-ideas of itself, an organic human being in an objective, material universe. There is simply no other mind or thinking entity present especially a lying, vicious one to suggest or argue anything to harm or entice you into its dream of false, hypnotic beliefs and illusions. Doing this will simultaneously generate the awareness and conviction of the truth and the good feelings of oneness, perfection, peace, fearless security and love. You now have the necessary weapons or tools to reveal the harmony and perfection you seek and these tools are "knowing" the truth and "feeling" the love, perfection and reality of this truth. You have the realization of the truth. When this *realization* of the truth is successfully done with a firm conviction, this will, in turn, remove the hypnotic clouds of mistaken beliefs and fear and reveal through that refocused lens, what was always there, the comforting awareness of a unity of Being where health, peace, abundance, harmony and true Living is your eternal experience.[122]

On the other hand, on the imagined human hand where identity theft took place, the blind belief of being a separate, alien, so-called thinking ego is a vulnerable position from the start. Mistakenly believing to be a separate human ego immediately and automatically results in the hypnotic illusion and lies that one's life, happiness and fulfillment consists of and is dependent upon a finite material body with a separate, matter-based intelligence and that this life and body lives in and is dependent upon a finite material environment where it starts life by being born but then must inevitably die. This believed separateness and physicality instantly generates a false sense of vulnerability to all the so-called "physical laws" and objective causes that now may be violated knowingly or unknowingly and seem to be outside of your full control. This false sense, this erring belief of vulnerability[123] is *fear,* a negative feeling, and if intense enough and coupled with a focus upon the very threat that is feared, whether specific or not, will hypnotically manifest the very thing that is feared.[124]

The error of manifesting hypnotic, negative effects or experiences in your life is always by the same process, by believing that you are a *separate* ego, a *separate,* human ego, whose thinking can only be mistakes and lies, the imagined mind and imagined body that will eventually be revealed and destroyed. A liar who, through its inevitable erroneous beliefs about many inharmonious, objective causes, makes its imaginary presence known to your false ego as an objective person, place, thing or condition. In the very same proportion that you believe this false nightmare of many *separate,* thinking causes, of many objective intelligences to be true and outside the one and only Consciousness and harmonious, thinking cause - that same level of negative feeling and fear will now reside within the imagined you, the victimized human ego in a dream. When this "knowing" of the lie or ill-effect is believed to be true and is coupled with the "feeling" or fear that it is true and together, if of sufficient conviction and belief, will manifest in your hypnotic nightmare the very lie or false suggestion that you feared real in the first place.[125]

Fear and false belief in "possibilities"

Also, if a strong sense of general vulnerability or fear (feeling) is present without specifically detailing or outlining (knowing) the threat feared, this blind, negative sense may still be hypnotically manifested as some negative malady in your experience. This is because the required knowing element, although not specific at that time, can still tap into, if any are present, negative possibilities, lies or ill-effects within the false ego's belief-mind and memory of erring convictions conjured up by the hypnotic belief of being outside the one, infinite Consciousness and being a separate and independently thinking consciousness - a material, thinking organism in a vulnerable material universe of many inharmonious causes. This false knowing element together with the false feeling element of fear generated from the general sense of vulnerability, will again manifest a negative experience, a so-called "random" ill-effect and nightmare according to these erring but firm convictions that may be quietly sitting there as a "real possibility" in one's life. Of course, just the opposite will take place when the true facts of one's true Being are realized and contemplated as I AM *individually* the Identity and awareness of the only Consciousness, cause and presence there is and AM entirely harmonious and perfect. In this realization of perfect oneness, a true feeling of love, peace and perfection of wakened reality is continuously sensed and good things "randomly happen," that is, an infinite quantity of harmonious effects and ideas are revealed to have always been there.[126]

All conditions and experiences - real, good and true ideas or false, bad and untrue illusion-ideas - come into our lives upon this two-element mechanism consisting of knowing either the true idea or the opposing lie to be real, and the associated feeling of either love and harmony about the true idea or fear that the opposing lie and illusion is real. Remember, we are each in our own, individual mental universe where the only creative power that is consciousness, will automatically cause, manifest and reflect one's convictions whether good or bad (i.e. health or sickness, wealth or poverty, happiness or unhappiness, harmonious or chaotic working conditions, relationships, governments, etc.), subjectively within itself, the great blackboard, computer output or movie screen of life experience.[127] For any phenomena to be manifested, whether true, good ones or bad, erroneous ones, they both require the knowing element and the matching feeling element in consciousness to be present. Remove either one (both preferably), either the knowing element or the feeling element and the specific manifestation cannot occur because the conviction, true or false, is no longer sound and firm. In a sense, knowing can be likened to the male element and feeling to the female element, both of which must be united to reveal any manifestation.[128]

Health, wealth, and happiness are always present in the realization of the infinite I AM, so let's take the ample supply of money as an example. An ample supply of money and its intelligent use to meet all your needs is goodness indeed! Acknowledging and fearing a hypnotic lack of money, a lack of goodness as a real condition only perpetuates it, so this conviction must be dropped immediately. But, simply *knowing* the true thought that supply is always abundant and any manifestation of lack is a specific unreal and opposing illusion about this fact is a right start but will not do much in revealing and uncovering the true state of ample supply. To reveal the true condition of abundant supply where a lack seems to be, the addition of a correct *feeling* that this thought is true must be simultaneously entertained, i.e. fearless, true feelings of abundance, peace, fulfillment, love and perfection, must be added to this correct and accurate *knowing*. This correct conviction present in your conscious awareness and realization of your oneness with Good, with the infinite, abundant, harmonious Being reveals your ever present true state and wins the battle.

Familiarity with true Identity

Now is the time to become familiar with your true, fearless and loving Identity, your true "I AM," and sharpen your skills in detecting the separate, idiotic, false, lying identity and the mechanism by which it seeks to gain its "life" and hypnotic nightmare of misery, lack, unhappiness, sickness, deceit, and death for you.[129] Always remember, garbage in, garbage out. You can now take advantage of understanding how all phenomena, that is really your sense and conviction of yourself, are all revealed and manifested through this knowing and feeling mechanism, the only creative engine there is by watching and insisting that your knowing and feeling are of the facts - the harmonious, intelligent truth that you are aware of self as the one infinite Consciousness that is the only creator there is with the joyful feeling of perfection and reality at all times. Furthermore, this truth is simply not that you are a mental being entirely composed of consciousness for the separate alien ego can also claim this, but that you are *INDIVIDUALLY* the ONLY CONSCIOUS *SELF* TO REVEAL THE ONENESS OF INFINITE LIFE AND PERFECTION ALWAYS. Through the joyful thoughts and feelings of oneness, love and perfection, I AM will be revealed as positive, perfect conditions that always existed like the sun after the imaginary clouds of adverse conditions disappear or watching a movie after the lens gets properly focused again.[130]

The freedom of choice has always been ours, but we never knew it would be on such an encompassing, universal scale. Through intelligent reasoning you can now know, feel and realize the truth that you have absolutely nothing to fear, for you are the only true Being in existence. You *individually* are the one, infinite Consciousness that is the *only* perfect cause and your awareness of your perfect Self is the *only* perfect effect.[131] Both the cause and the effect are always directly linked and are infinite, good, complete, perfect, abundant, harmonious, eternal, and one. There is only one Identity in existence and this is the only *individual* there is, the only I, Intelligence and Good.[132] Meditate, practice, and more actively understand and sense reality by continuously knowing the truth and feeling the love of one, infinite, impersonal, perfect Being. Focus on the correct Identity of your true Self that is, I AM, through accurate reasoning, knowing and feeling.[133] In so doing, the reversed, distorted, hypnotic, derivative lies and finite illusion-ideas generated by the imagined, separate and mistaken, fearful human ego will flee like cockroaches when a light is turned on.[134] Cut through the imaginary, hypnotic fabric of an inharmonious and finite material so-called reality with the actual, true reality of the infinite presence that was always there.

As you practice reasoning and holding to the truth, to the wonderful facts about your true oneness of Being, the resultant, false and fearful evidence of so-called material laws, causes, forces, proclivities and other negative "realities" that victimize you in your hypnotic, physical, big bang universe-dream will diminish in proportion to the strength and accuracy of your conviction. The so-called finite, physical, objective universe containing numerous inharmonious minds and causes everywhere and all its so-called random challenges, limitations, distractions, and disasters was never a thing or a reality to contend with. It was only the resultant illusory mental phenomena, hypnotic lies, and nightmares logically generated from this insidious identity thief, the erroneous belief of being a separate, human ego, who is itself, a liar.

A single universe

There never was a duality of universes to contend with, one being a true, factual universe of one Being and the other a physical, finite, objective universe. The so-called physical universe of separated, finite ideas and minds simply never existed outside of its own hypnotic illusion. As in the movie projector analogy given previously, it was simply nothing but an out of focus lens projecting a lie, an illusion, a dream and a distorted nightmare that reversed the true facts about the single, true universe and this dream will be wakened from and forgotten. The false illusion-idea of a finite, physical, objective universe that resulted from the old and mistaken individual belief of being a separate, human ego and identity is simply a misinterpretation of the true image and likeness of the one Intelligence and Ego. You will see the false, inharmonious shadows simply dissolve as you reason, understand and live the true conviction, the true realization and feeling that YOU ARE I AM. You are now the awareness of Self as the one infinite

Consciousness, the only celestial Being in existence where your body is the entire universe that is always perfect and good to the exclusion of and in forgetting that old liar. Forget that imagined and imposing, false, dreamlike identity separated and outside reality that is aware of its false self as "i am a finite human being, the separate ego living in the dream and illusion of a very limited lifespan bounded within a meat-sack body and a birth-life-death sequence in a finite, material universe." As this correct understanding is gained, the awareness of your true Identity of one, infinite, Consciousness expressed as one perfect universe will be revealed as you remember you have always been there and have never left.[135]

Celestial hints re-present the truth

Along with the sun being obscured by clouds in an example previously given, the sun, Earth and moon and their relationships with one another also re-presents exactly what this book is attempting to explain. In this example, the sun, and there is only one, represents consciousness, the only cause and creative engine which possesses all the mental energy and activity that can illuminate and reveal either true ideas or false illusions. The sun is the primary entity, the singular and sole creative power and in an orderly manner, holds the whole solar system in its grasp. It is the center of the solar system and its "offspring" are the planets of varying identities that revolve around it. Without the sun, nothing is illuminated or energized, nothing is seen or known and no identity or awareness consisting of either true facts or false beliefs is revealed and manifested. Until sunlight (life, consciousness) is reflected by something (expressing a true idea or false illusion), the sun's rays, or cause, and the generic ideas they reveal are invisible or unknown. So there, in the sphere of influence of the creative engine of the sun, of consciousness, we have two "things," two effects reflecting life, two images and likenesses, two identities to examine. One revealed identity, the spherical Earth, symbolizes the true and correct reflected idea or effect of the one, whole Ego and Life, the only true individual - Intelligence. The other revealed identity, the spherical moon, symbolizes and reflects the imagined and deranged idea and effect of the separate, alien ego, the cause of the illusion of human existence, desolation and death. Both need the sun (life, consciousness) as an energizing, illuminating power for their respective ideas and effects to be reflected or be revealed (known and aware). Both are spheres symbolizing the law of universal creativity of effect exactly reflecting cause in individual being, whether that identity is reflecting the true Ego or the false, alien ego.[136]

The correct idea and identity, the one Ego and Life represented and reflected by Earth fully reveals all sides of itself to the illuminating power of the sun by revolving on its axis every twenty-four hours. It has nothing to hide and abundantly makes itself known and available for enjoyment. The manifestation of the beautiful blue Earth, lighted, warmed, and energized by the sun, makes itself known and is aware of its true individual Identity and Life by reflecting all its abundance, perfection and goodness. This becomes all the more significant and amazing when we consider that within the vastness of cold, dark and empty space we have this beautiful, nurturing Earth teeming with abundant life of enormous variety. Most importantly among this abundant life expression lies the absolute crown of creation and consciousness - the conscious awareness of self! Rational consciousness actually aware of its own self! In addition, all the good attributes and meanings of the structure of Earth and the variety of things that live there collectively contribute their share to represent and reflect the Identity and self-awareness of the infinite, one Being, the one Life, the true Identity, always abundant, beautiful, perfect and good.

On the other hand, the moon represents and reflects the identity, manifestation or illusion-idea of the separate, alien, ego. The moon is desolate with absolutely no life resident in or on the bodily structure of that sphere. All the attributes of the moon are collectively those of the separate, alien ego - stark, barren and lifeless. In perfectly accurate symbolism, the latest theory of the origin of the moon shows it to have been blown out of and become "separated" from Earth after a collision with some "other" planetary body.[137]

Dark side of the moon

Also, in perfect symbolism, this representation of the separate, alien ego seems to have something to hide. The moon's rotational speed on its axis exactly matches the rotational speed of Earth so that as the moon revolves around Earth, the opposite side of the moon, the dark side, is never viewed from Earth. Isn't this a typical and leading characteristic that is required to support illusions, to hide and conceal the truth about the illusion that would render it a fake? Viewed from Earth, the lifeless moon even appears to be equal in size to the sun in its vain attempt to counterfeit the *only* energizing life and consciousness re-presented by the sun. Although trying to appear as a real, separate life or consciousness that resides in a so-called material body as erring human beliefs would have it, the only so-called life or consciousness that the moon has causing it to glow, is the energy already put there by the sun, the one and only impersonal life, consciousness and energy there is. The moon has no "glowing" ability, life or consciousness of its own just like the illusion of life residing in and dependent on a so-called material, physical body has no energizing life or intelligence of its own. The moon's limited, counterfeit, and false imitation of "life" is further demonstrated by its weak, cold, deathly glow compared to actual life and consciousness, the sun - bright and warm. Here we now see why the alien ego, the moon, is always hiding its dark side. To go around to the dark side we would see that the moon is not glowing at all and does not possess consciousness or life of its own. We see that the moon is a fake, a counterfeit, and has no glowing, illuminating, or life-giving powers of its own. The moon feebly attempts the illusion that it does contain life by stealing light and life from the sun, the only life and consciousness there is.

Life cycles of the moon

When viewed from Earth, the moon also symbolizes the inevitable cycles of life that occur when one finds oneself as a separate, alien ego, the human ego. Perfectly re-presenting the resultant separate, alien ego's birth-life-death cycles, the moon's life is born, waxes and matures to full strength that we see as the full moon, and then wanes and declines to its inevitable demise and disappearance only to reappear and repeat the process again endlessly. In this endless, deathly cycle, first we see the moon, very small as a sliver and hardly noticeable, sharing the wakened day with the sun, representing the true Identity and Life in this example. In darkness where sleep and dreams dominate, the moon's life and identity become more noticeable. As the moon's so-called life or cause progresses to maturity, its respective ideas or effects are soon revealed. What was once the beautiful, bright, colorful Earth, the only real, reflected Life as revealed by the sun, the only true cause, we now have the false effect of a false, alien cause that is now reflected by a shabby, weak, dark and colorless Earth as revealed by the moon's weak and deathly glow. Again, the separate, alien ego symbolized by the full moon, is attempting to imitate the one and only Life there is that is symbolized by the sun. In its feeble attempt, and along with its apparent equal size from an observer on Earth, it is trying to appear as another consciousness, another life, another identity and another energizing and illuminating ego - the separate alien ego. Its only energizing life or consciousness is really from the sun but it mistakenly and absurdly claims to have its own, separate, energizing life as evidenced by its counterfeit glow.[138] Occurring only at night and in darkness that are prime conditions for dreams and nightmares, its brief but fullest glory of a full moon rises above the horizon just as the sun, the only Life - Intelligence is "disappearing" at sunset. This is perfect timing, because the imagined human ego, in its identity theft of the true Ego, is in its top form of death and destruction when intelligence, truth and love are suppressed the most. Subsequent nights following its brief night of "glory" we see it disintegrating and once again, being dominated by and chased away by the warm, morning sun - the only Intelligence and Life. The brighter the testimony of Intelligence becomes, the fainter becomes the moon's claim.

In time the moon diminishes, disappears and "dies" but no sooner is it gone, that we see it "born" in the sky again, only to repeat its carbon-copy, birth-life-death sequences again and again. Not only does this illustrate the folly of claiming to be a separate intelligence or a separate, thinking cause that will always be condemned to the reflected illusions and nightmares of birth-life-death phases and cycles that is really not Life at all, but especially of the tenacious nature of erring convictions that remain uncorrected - they just keep repeating themselves endlessly until corrected.

To top this off, we even have the identity of the "man in the moon" or what looks like a human face when the moon is at or near full. During a lunar eclipse when Earth blocks the sun, there also seems to be the image of a woman's face and hair looking to one side on the moon. Truly the identities of "human beings in the moon" and all the while hiding and concealing the dark side! Then there is the example of the solar eclipse where the moon, the separate, alien ego, in its outrageous and nightmarish insolence, attempts to block out Consciousness or Life completely with total darkness as in a mistaken human belief of death and confusion, in its brief, and always unsuccessful, attempted identity theft of the one, indestructible, Life and Consciousness.[139]

Solar energy

In another representation, it can be shown that almost all energy related activities on Earth can be classified as originating from the sun, or consciousness to restate the analogy. All weather - the wind, the rain and snow, rivers, etc., are energized by the sun. Energy sources such as coal, petroleum, natural gas, wood, geothermal, hydro and wind tur-bines, and solar cells are all energized by solar energy with various storage times. The movement and activity of all creatures is fueled by organic food which food can also be traced back to the sun as its energy source. All energy related activities on Earth can be traced back to the sun in one way or another.

Technically, a form of nuclear energy is directly related to the sun as in the case of nuclear fusion that is the same process that powers the sun and the stars. It is worth noting that nuclear fission, that is, the split-ting apart or *separating* the structure of the uranium atom results in a very problematic form of power. The process can readily be turned into weapons making activities, power plant accidents can be catastrophic and spent fuel is highly toxic, lasts for thousands of years and has to be buried or carefully stored. Its benefits are very similar to the problem-atic, separate, alien ego that conjured it up. Nuclear fusion on the other hand, that is the *uniting* of hydrogen atoms to form a helium atom that naturally occurs on the sun and the stars, promises an almost limitless, safe and clean source of energy although not technologically feasible as of this writing. At present rates of global energy consumption, it is es-timated that enough fuel, deuterium, exists in the oceans to power the planet for billions of years.[140] I would hazard to predict that at the same time the truth and oneness of Being is more generally understood and practiced globally, that is, the uniting of mankind with his and her true Identity, that nuclear fusion power will come into greater fruition.[141] The alien ego will simply not permit the depletion or polluting use of fossil fuels to interfere with the continuation of the human race to go racing on…to where? Other than endless birth-life-death cycles, it-knows-not-where nor cares where as long as its idiotic cycles keep going on.

In short, all energy and activity is driven by the one and only source: consciousness that is symbolized by the sun. It is worth noting that no such carbon cycle or energy storage and release mechanism, except for the sun's warmth imparted to its surface during the day exists on the moon that symbolizes that lifeless alien; the separate ego im-postor.

Of course, there are more re-presentations and symbolic scenarios in celestial Earth, moon, and sun relationships like solar eclipses, night and day, ocean tides, rainbows, solar winds, stars, galaxies, black holes, and the like, but I'll let the reader interpret these and other celestial re-presentations quietly hinting to our true, harmonious state of affairs.

Chapter 6

Death of the Big Bang Universe

It has been reasoned that only one, impersonal, infinite, universal Mind exists in reality. It was concluded that this infinite Mind is perfect Intelligence where this only Consciousness in existence is aware only of itself *individually* as the sole, infinite I AM. There is simply nothing else to be aware of other than itself. This knowing and feeling of its complete, infinite, perfect self, that is, its active, conscious and *individual* awareness of itself consisting of all perfect attributes and meanings, is the only manifested impersonal universe or body of ideas there is. The infinite Mind does not contain infinite *separate* individuals, as erring human beliefs would have it, but rather knows itself as one individual in an infinite manner. It individually knows no *separateness*. Similarly, the infinite number of rays of the sun all express one sun. Each ray identifies and enjoys itself as the *expression* of the whole entirety of the sun. In the same way that the rays, that are many, are not the sun, so too individual awareness reveals, expresses, and reflects, the infinite idea that infinite Intelligence has available.

A hypnotic dream of an illusory, counterfeit, objective universe consisting of separate egos, separate beings, fear, vulnerability, inharmonious causes, finite forms, material substances and undesirable qualities, are all separated and unknown to the infinite awareness. "I AM infinite Intelligence, the only harmonious cause and Identity and my individual awareness of myself reveals the only manifestation, expression, reflection or universe there is." The so-called objective, physical universe has been reasoned to be the resultant, erroneous, dreamlike, hypnotic effect and faulty idea caused to appear by an erroneous concept and belief of being a separate, alien ego, outside of the one perfect Consciousness, that in our personal experience, is the human ego. This erroneously supposed and suggested, separate, human ego cannot be real. It is simply an imagined illusion, and both this "liar" and its so-called "creative thinking" can only result in aggressive, hypnotic, nightmarish lies and failures that attempt to hide and usurp reality and must be destroyed. This can only be accomplished through intelligent reasoning. It can't be wished away, we do not naturally grow out of it and it does not magically disappear by dying or any other mistaken, "whacked-out" concepts and beliefs. Only by truly understanding the nature of the alien ego and its insidious process of identity theft, can we subdue and destroy this hypnotic criminal intruder and waken from its worthless, *dead-ended* dream.

Evidence of separate ego prior to human evolution

The erroneous claim and inharmonious manifestations of a separate, alien ego did not start with the evolution of a separate, human ego, although that is where we experienced the false, hypnotic dream. The false claim or erring belief of an impersonal, *separate, alien* ego started prior to the evolution of human or any other "objective" rational being, and was instantly manifested as an erroneous reflection or mistaken and hypnotic awareness of itself as the beginning of the objective, big bang universe (lower case intentional). The universal law of mind's creative activity can never be annulled. Effect instantly and continuously reflects cause. This imagined, false claim of an impersonal ego *separated* from the one and only, infinite Ego, is automatically expressed and manifested subjectively in consciousness, the great blackboard or movie screen of any creation, as the beginning of the hypnotic dream of a so-called, objective, big bang universe-phenomena. This imagined and nightmarish, impersonal, separate, alien ego with all its distorted illusions, lies and absence of true Life (death) certainly did not start with the human or rational being, but through intelligent reasoning that shines forth and exposes its imagined and mistaken "evolved self" - the human being - it will certainly end there.

Misinterpretation of I AM the Truth

The imagined and erroneous claim of being an impersonal, separate, alien ego misinterpreted and distorted the true idea of I AM, the only true universe, body or expression of I AM there is. This erroneous claim automatically results in a counterfeit reality consisting of the illusion-idea of a big bang phenomena where various, limiting "laws" and causes of objective physicality, finite time and evolution seem to be operating within the "life" portion of this illusory universe's own birth-life-death cycle. Due to the *infinite and eternal* nature of intelligent facts, illusions will be finite and of limited duration. They will always have a start, a maturation, and certainly an ending - death. Illusions and dreams that are not reality cannot go on indefinitely. As explained earlier, all the effects or ideas conceived by a *separate* mind believing itself to exist in addition to or outside of the only Mind and reality there is, perfect Intelligence, can only be *separated illusion*-ideas that are outside reality and must be lies and distortions about the only facts there are. These illusion-ideas that are separate and outside the true and harmonious facts or effects of Intelligence, are hypnotic dreams and consist of: separate, objective places (objective space) in lieu of I AM the only place; separate and finite substances (matter) in lieu of I AM the only substance; separate finite forms (things) in lieu of I AM an infinite form, that is, I do not dwell in nor harbor silly, limiting and multiple finite forms; separate inharmonious causes and laws (material life-systems and phenomena) in lieu of I AM the only harmonious cause and law, and separate limited, life-qualities (a life dead to the truth while living in a troublesome, death-oriented birth-life-death cycle) in lieu of I AM a whole, perfect, and eternal Life. Every idea imagined by this separate mind must have started with a perfect, harmonious idea that is then inharmoniously reversed. It has no other choice as there are no other ideas or meanings to distort and reverse. The additional and *separate* alien mind seems to be attempting to re-think or re-invent ideas in a field of an infinite quantity of already existing perfect ideas. It seems to be attempting to reach the coveted stature of "creator" that it can never do in reality, only in childish, make-believe, immature illusions. The only available ideas generated in this imagined mind are inharmonious, imperfect counterfeits and reversed illusions of the harmonious truth - the out of focus lens in the movie projector analogy previously given. Instead of an infinite and complete Being, the alien claims its universe must evolve from some distant beginning that automatically implies an inevitable end. Its "new," faulty, counterfeit ideas that are really illusions always require a starting point followed by a maturation or evolution segment that all lead to the only end point or conclusion that a mistaken counterfeit cause and its illusion-ideas will ever reach; death and destruction. Illusions are never real and must always end eventually. The resultant effects or derivatives of this imagined, separate ego position began as the illusion-ideas of objective space, energy, and matter, which are, of course, the counterfeit big bang universe. Later on in the evolution of this fake, objective, material universe when the rational organic being "evolved," it has provided its own illusory evidence and history to the human being's befooled senses by way of the out of focus lens analogy. With our erring human reasoning based on these befooled and hypnotized senses (all based on false, material beliefs of separateness), we have erroneously concluded that an objective physical universe we are witness to is the truth and has evolved in time through various stages of separate and finite galaxies, stars, planets, gases, liquids, solids, bacteria, animals, etc., all the way up to the rational being who, in our case on Earth, is the human being and ego. It must be kept in mind that the material big bang phenomena and its evolutionary universe all the way up to the human being did *seem to happen*, because right now we do *seem to be in it* - but only as a false illusion, an overshadowing hypnotic, dream that is never reality.[142] Although most may not know it, we are still dealing with and residing within the actual, real and harmonious universe and body of the only Being there is, I AM ALL - nothing else exists. Through a distorting, out of focus lens we see our life experience on the screen of subjective consciousness as a human being in a material, objective universe that "some creator" has made.

Ultimate goal of error

Through this illusory lens, all the seemingly evolutionary and lesser phenomena of this separate, impersonal, deadly, alien ego prior to the evolution of its highest phenomena, the rational being, were rather dramatic displays of explosions, collisions, black holes and other astronomical phenomena, and the like that seem to continue on to this day. However dramatic these galactic occurrences may have been and continue to be, they all must seem quite dull and mechanical compared to the incredible disasters, suffering, horrors and death that can now be *personally experienced* when higher levels of separate self-conscious awareness and rational beings have evolved within the illusion. Hate, fear, starvation, greed, pride, jealousy, lust, murder, suicide, war, polarizing cultural and religious beliefs, confusion, vulnerability in an aging meat-sack body, frustration, loneliness, helplessness, depression and substance abuse are just a few of the false beliefs, lies and failures that the evolved human ego can assign to itself as a direct result of believing to be a separate ego along with its attendant lies and seemingly infinite, inharmonious causes.[143] Instinctively in its efforts to enjoy more of life, to feel more secure in increased health, wealth, and happiness, the hypnotized human ego is continuously searching for good and harmony in the only place it knows of, objective physicality believed to be real and outside of its true self, Consciousness. Tragically the search for more good in one's life is restrained to the hypnotic, belief-realm of objective illusion-ideas, where eventually, they begin to see that permanent happiness and goodness will never be found there. Sadly and unknown to the unfortunate, hypnotized individual, the objective universe and the human body is an illusion, a fake counterfeit. Unfulfilled disappointment and inharmonious experiences will increasingly attend every searching exercise for happiness and fulfillment until one's soul starts to question the validity of the search and the search-field itself. It is at this point in the individual's struggle where these fertile and enticing fields of false promises become the battlefields of truth versus lies.

Reasoning reveals the enemy

It is upon these false and promising fertile fields of lies and illusions, where all the inharmonious experiences, sufferings, confusion and death of the human's *life* will occur. It is here, seemingly constrained within this hypnotic nightmare, where the evolved intelligence of the rational ego will eventually be forced to work and reason about the cause of these adverse conditions in its efforts to finally be rid of them. The battles of fact versus fiction, intelligence versus false beliefs goes on in their reasoning until they finally discover that the real enemy responsible for the inharmonious experiences and limitations is not a so-called objective universe with material people, places, things, laws, causes, forces, passions and other constraints and limitations beyond their control for there are none, *but that it is an aggressive and very creative enemy inadvertently allowed within their own mind unawares.*[144] Through reasoning they discover the *only enemy ever*, is found to be an impersonal, fake, alien mind mistakenly claiming to be their own self and identity as a separate consciousness outside of the infinite, singular, perfect Consciousness. An aggressive, imposing, counterfeit mind and ego who has hidden the true Identity of the one, infinite, celestial, Intelligence by superimposing an ignorant mind, an imaginary mind, a dying mind - the fearful, separate, human, alien mind over the real Mind and sole Identity of eternal Life, perfection and love. This impostor masquerading as your "self" and identity is now forced because of its own believed *separateness* to view existence through a distorting lens and it becomes, through the law of cause and effect, a liar dead to the truth. This imaginary mind, this alien ego mistakenly suggests, argues for and simultaneously believes that counterfeit, inharmonious, hypnotic, illusion-ideas seen and experienced through the out of focus lens are real - like the good, perfect and true facts it has inadvertently distorted.[145] In direct proportion to the amount of inharmonious lies that are believed to be true by the individual, they will appear to hypnotically live, suffer and die in them as the automatic consequences of an inharmonious, illusory, objective universe they themselves have inadvertently created. Life as a so-called human being is only a hypnotic dream but it will contain all the failures, terror, fear, false pleasures and confusion of a nightmare that is believed to be real until you waken from the dream and erring beliefs that form it. Finally the individual has found the power and the weapon to end the failures of this suffering, illusion filled nightmare in the same way that intelligence has found the power to solve problems and failures in all other arenas - the power and weapon of intelligent reasoning to understand the true nature of the challenge and conquer it.

Justice of universal Consciousness

In the absolutely just and fair universal creative law of life - individual consciousness, true or false, always automatically shows itself to itself as its individual awareness of itself corresponding exactly to its own conviction of the "facts" it feels are true about anything including its individual self and identity. This individual conviction of *what is real* and its automatic, subjective reflection, shadow or awareness (its individually expressed universe), is purely a one to one relationship. It is quite mechanical in this respect as you are the only one directing your experience and *you own all of it*! Whether based on true facts or false beliefs, this revealing mechanism always automatically links individual consciousness and its reflected individual convictions expressed subjectively as its *exact man*ifestation or awareness of itself.[146] Like the movie theater analogy made earlier, the medium of consciousness is like a projecting light source of a movie projector and the film passing through it are the harmonious facts of Being that, when properly focused with the lens of correct understanding and viewpoint, will be revealed onto the screen of individual Life and experience to be harmoniously enjoyed. There is no other subject film available than the true facts of Being. Only facts, certainty and reality are present on the film of Truth. $2 + 2 = 4$, harmony, health and peace will be present but $2 + 2 = 7$ or 9, confusion, sickness, death or any other inharmonious mistake will not be. The only part of the projector we have any influence over, and thereby our projected life experience thrown onto the screen, is the lens representing our understanding or erroneous beliefs of what is true and what is not true respectively. Our convictions affect the focus of the *individual* projector lens directly. Any conviction, whether correct understanding or mistaken and false beliefs will define the setting of the lens and the projector will automatically project an identical image to express or reflect what the conviction itself is. Although what looks to be real, finite and material things, places and persons on the screen of our life experience at this time, we know it is nothing more than the inanimate expression of an incorrect and out of focus lens setting (our erring convictions as to what is believed true) reversing and distorting the facts of Being contained on the film. It is again noted that the projected image of true facts or false illusions, are still energized or thrown off by the power of the intense light - consciousness. When individual mind correctly understands itself to be the one and only impersonal, infinite Consciousness of love and perfection whose presence and meaning is everyone, everything, everywhere and there is nothing else, the lens is properly focused. However, when individual mind mistakenly and hypnotically believes itself to be one of many finite, separated, thinking, organic human egos that are mere specks in a finite material universe, the lens is way out of focus and the true image and likeness seeking expression are reversed, distorted and upside down. Therefore, individual mind will automatically project forth, reflect and *man*ifest a full expression or universe of itself to itself as its awareness of itself in direct accordance with its own convictions of itself. This is a just and fair law of creation and process of revealing one way or another, the only universe of Life we ever had, subjective, universal Consciousness. Your universe is *you* reflected back to you exactly to correspond to the amount of understanding or blind, erroneous beliefs you hold to be true. You are always the one impersonal, invisible and universal consciousness, the only cause, and your awareness or belief in your convictions of self and identity, true or false, will always be subjectively and exactly manifested as your entire universe, the effect and expression. You are always this one mind and your body is always manifested as this one universe, *man* (the *man* in manifestation) whether understood and seen correctly or not. Effect or manifestation will always automatically reflect its cause exactly as they are always one in this respect.[147] Therefore, in the case of the one true, impersonal, infinite, Consciousness, it will automatically shadow forth, reflect, cause and manifest a full expression, body and universe of itself to itself as its conviction of itself. In revealing the complete, infinite Being of Life, truth, love and perfection, it is truly revealing the true image and likeness of Intelligence - *man*.[148] Likewise, in the case of identity theft by the *separate*, alien human ego, the liar with its suggested lies, it too will automatically shadow forth, reflect, reveal and manifest a full but hypnotic, illusory expression, body and universe of itself to itself as its conviction of itself.[149] But in that illusion and reversal of the truth, instead of your impersonal body being revealed subjectively as the entire impersonal universe of eternal good, love and perfection, you will hypnotically appear as a separated ego, subjectively expressed as a separate, finite, material being vaguely residing as and within a vulnerable, fearful and personal meat-sack body in a separated, physical, objective universe subject to all the seemingly infinite, separate, inharmonious causes and their respective problems and failures all framed within the matter-based, birth-life-death cycles found there. Quite a contrast![150]

The entire expression or mental manifestation (subjectively within consciousness of course, for there is no other type of image, likeness, shadow, reflection, expression, phenomena, idea or manifestation), whether they be true ideas or false illusion-ideas, are always automatically projected or revealed exactly according to your convictions (lens setting) subjectively on the movie screen of life experience. You do, in fact, whether aware of it or not, always express yourself as a complete individual universe, entirely and subjectively within what is actually, the *only* creative engine of creation - impersonal, universal consciousness constantly operating or reflecting throughout the forever *now* of eternity. Your universe, all of it and whatever that universe may entail and whatever condition it is in, is the exact reflection of you, *always* because it is *only you* who has created it!

There is only one Ego and this one Life is enjoyed as its awareness of all its perfection and goodness unless distorted by identity theft by the imagined alien ego. Just like the movie projector analogy previously given, there will always be only one fixed projector, only one fixed projector light, only one fixed film reel of the truth and one *variable* lens to focus properly or improperly according to our correct understanding or erring beliefs onto the individual screen of life experience. Therefore the universe, whether clearly focused through understanding the oneness of Being or out of focus through the false convictions of a separate ego will always be one universe. One universe that can either be seen and enjoyed correctly or seen as a distorted counterfeit believed to be true.

There will always be the just universal creative law of one individual mind and its corresponding universe revealing that mind's convictions. By replacing false ones through sound reasoning, so too in pure justice, do the erroneous, hypnotic illusions and nightmares of a separate, objective big bang universe and all its numerous, separate, forms, substances, minds and inharmonious failures fade from experience and reveal the individual unity and Identity of the one, perfect, infinite, *individual* Mind and Life as the true and only universe.[151]

Progressive advancement and resultant benefits

Just as we have progressively advanced step by step in all other subject areas, so too will our advancement here be a step-by-step logical progression. Some individuals will be drawn to and grasp this understanding sooner than others.[152] Others will actively apply their clear understanding with little wandering back to prior false beliefs and naturally reap the benefits of increased health, wealth and happiness through dominating and controlling ignorance and erroneous beliefs.[153] Through it all, we all have varying degrees of erroneous and aggressive thought habits to battle and contend with. Whatever the case may be, no one will reach and waken out of the human induced illusion in an instant. Whatever rate of progress is most comfortable and harmonious for each individual will rule the day. For others, they may not be interested in this endeavor at this time.[154] Some may even ridicule and mock[155] this reasoning and understanding as being contrary and worthless compared to the presently accepted, "modern" teachings and beliefs of human beings in the medical, religious and cultural fields among others[156] but this does not matter, as it is all based on individual inspiration and choice.[157] For example, does an accomplished musician, artist, engineer or scientist miraculously reach their level of expertise instantaneously without diligent study, effort and practice of their craft? Does a child instantaneously reach adulthood or does an acorn when placed in a nutrient rich environment instantaneously become the sturdy oak? Work, patience, and joyful progress have always been the keys to these achievements and those keys apply here as well. Typically one's health is the first area to be addressed. Start with what you think are the simpler problems and as you practice and get results, your confidence will increase to handle "harder" problems and on up the line. Of course, no problem is any harder than any other problem when it is fully understood that they are all simply erring convictions of the existence of an erroneous separate mind opposing the harmonious truth with lies and illusions all of which are impossible. The work of intelligent reasoning will reach increased levels of understanding and a better ability to detect subtle, hypnotic illusions, false beliefs and fear will ensue. This better understanding of the facts is now actively, joyously and continuously known and felt instead of the former false beliefs and fears.[158] In the same measure that this is done, will your entire universe gradually reveal your new convictions and reward you for work well done.[159] After all, the *entire universe* and all it contains is simply the reflection of *your beliefs* and *your convictions,* not something or someone else's.[160] The entire universe and all the ideas in it that you are conscious of are yours and yours alone whether interpreted correctly or not. There is only one individual Mind and its projected image of itself, and this projected image that is thrown up on that neutral screen is always composed of your convictions, whether correct or not. Only you can maintain its harmonious reality that is revealed to have always been there like the sun and the film reel, or introduce the clouds and out of focus, inharmonious conditions of a *separated,* illusion state. Just as in all other arenas, correct understanding is a tool that must be applied and utilized to accomplish the task. Only through casting out and correcting false beliefs by constantly replacing them with the true facts that are reached and supported by intelligent reasoning, can this work be accomplished. For this to occur, the yearning for truth must be sincere, honest, and genuine. We, you, us - the mistaken "many minds" and identities are simply journeying from the erroneous many who were enveloped in the hypnotic and unreal illusion of a ghastly, material and separate sense of ego and a birth-life-death sequence, to arrive at our true Identity in reality - the one, whole individual, harmonious, eternal, infinite, Consciousness of love and perfection that resides everywhere.

Foolish attempts to "trick" creative mechanism

It will be foolish indeed, to attempt to manifest and satisfy any wrong human desire with this method while truly knowing in one's heart, that the desire, no matter how closely cherished by the hypnotized human ego, is a selfish, erroneous belief. Also, it will be found to be equally foolish to manifest a good experience while knowingly harboring these erroneous beliefs, feelings and desires.[161] Again, in pure justice, individual consciousness can never be a hypocrite to itself. It may try to fool others but it can never fool itself. Whatever is within will be exactly and genuinely shadowed forth subjectively without.[162] All inharmonious, uneasy (dis-easy), untrue thoughts, feelings and convictions must be discarded, or depending on their intensity, will be shadowed forth in your body and experiences (your universe) in the same proportional degree. We all have a pretty good idea of what these uneasy thoughts, feelings and convictions are; hate, fear, jealousy, inordinate lust and greed, lack of friends, money, companionship, happiness, and understanding...lack of anything; negative beliefs in a million and one threats to one's health and harmonious being such as old age, contagion, allergies, inherited diseases, puffed up pride, blind ambition, unreasonable competitiveness, misery accumulation of wealth, cheating the unwary, resentment, hurt feelings, depression, enemies, troublesome neighbors, bad finances, economies, governments, leaders, etc., etc. These are all toxic lies and negative feelings that can and will mar your body and life experience in this dead, hypnotic dream of being a so-called separated ego in a so-called material, objective universe.

Dying accomplishes nothing

Only when the false, superimposing ego and liar is dissolved by corrected convictions through intelligent reasoning, can your true Mind and Being joyously shine forth as it always has the potential to do. Your eternal, infinite, pure and glorious understanding and awareness of the truth and perfection of you as I AM the one, perfect, infinite celestial Life will be seen to be superior to all imaginary and erroneous, negative beliefs to the contrary. Only by understanding the facts of your true Identity through reasoning, will this wonderful awareness of oneness, love, perfection and eternal Life shine forth. Dying will not do it. Dying cannot do it because dying is just one of the many suffering, hypnotic, illusion-ideas and failures that accomplish nothing but suffering. It does not add anything to one's understanding other than, hopefully, alerting oneself that an error exists. After all, it is the so-called objective universe and all it contains including our bodies that subjectively lives in us, consciousness, and not us, objective, physical beings living in an objective universe as previously believed in the reversed, upside-down illusion. In a manner of speaking, it is only the universe of false beliefs and erring ideas that has to worry about dying and being terminated, not the truth of Life. Individually making the mistake of $2 + 2 = 5, 7$ or 9 will never have any truth or reality status and this error believed true will eventually die - and so too will your erring convictions and beliefs, whatever they may be.

When one experiences the erring belief of so-called death in this human, hypnotic dream of existence, one's life will be seen to be continuous nevertheless - the movie theater never closes. Whatever other erring beliefs were cherished or feared (believed to be true) before death, they will still remain to be dealt with by the individual after this so-called death as the counterfeit life and false dream continues on.[163] Because these erring beliefs are simultaneously reflected or expressed in the universe we seem to "live in," one could "die" a million times and still find oneself suffering and laboring in the hypnotic dream of being a vulnerable and finite meat-sack in an objective, big bang universe of error and fear if these convictions of lies are not corrected by the truth and love of reality.[164] Because the universe always automatically expresses our convictions of the self and identity we believe to be, and the "truth" we believe to be true, it is not until the conviction of genuine Self and Truth are understood individually through intelligent reasoning, that an erroneous objective universe and negative experiences fades from view and you, the true, perfect universe, the Identity and self-awareness of one, Intelligence, Life, Truth and Love is once again revealed and shines through the illusion.[165] As in all other arenas we have mastered, mere beliefs in true facts will never be successful under the stress of circumstances or battle and this "thin ice" belief-position is only a rolling of the dice. Only solid understanding and a real sense of love, reached through intelligent reasoning will win the day.

Big bang and human history

Although in hypnotic human terms, human history seems quite long but relatively speaking, it is actually quite short when compared to the age of the big bang universe or age of Earth, estimated at approximately 15 billion and 4.5 billion years old respectively. Of course relatively speaking, even finite quantities like the age of the universe estimated at about 15 billion years could also appear to be quite short when compared to 15 trillion years or 15 nonillion years (that would be a 15 with 30 zeros after it!). When compared to the infinite, forever *now* of reality - that is eternal Life, the age of the big bang universe at 15 billion years (or even 15 nonillion years if there is such a universe) presents a very short, minuscule amount approaching and is nothing but a hypnotic dream. Basically, depending on where you are standing, the 15 billion year evolution-illusion of the big bang could have taken place in less than the blink of an eye, or a very long, laborious period of time, or simply in truth, not at all. The point here is to restate, from a different view, the *very limited,* finite nature of the subjective illusion-idea of a material universe. Hypnotic illusion-ideas can never contain reality, substance, Intelligence or Life of their own, shadows never can. Only the one, infinite, Intelligence can ever contain or be any of those real entities. It is the only Life-Engine there is.

All the relatively recent, evolutionary developments of human beings from cavemen to agricultural communities, increased communication, abstract thinking and the beginning of the age of reason, are all small steps of reasoning leading to this vital revelation and paradigm shift of what is fact and what is illusion on a universal scale. Religious struggles, scientific struggles, political struggles, technological struggles, cultural struggles, national struggles, economic struggles, etc, that all seemed so important in our brief history, were and are battles of truth versus false beliefs that we have worked through and have advanced in some cases, but not in all. But in a positive way, the pain and limitations of the resultant failures of false beliefs and convictions have forced us to engage our reasoning ability to understand the root cause of the failures that have so tenaciously ensnared us.[166]

All events and developments in the so-called objective universe leading up to this final war in the age of reason exposing the theft of our true Identity are rather insignificant compared to the point where we can understand the actual nature and falsehood of the big bang universe. In so doing, we can clearly see that it was simply a twisted dream, a hypnotic and distorted illusion that resulted from the identity theft of the one Ego and universe that was already there, I AM. Only in this way of intelligent reasoning by the individual, will the hypnotic illusion and nightmare of a finite, limited, physical, objective universe with all of its suffering and imagined, finite, separate egos die away in the individual's experience, to reveal the Identity of the one and only Being, the one and only individual and universe there ever was and ever will be - infinite and individual Consciousness, Intelligence, eternal Life, truth, love, perfection and good everywhere. A complete unity of Being. We are all IT, always have been, always will be, but we have somehow forgotten.[167] Exactly how we have forgotten our true Identity is unimportant at this time or at any time for it was only a hypnotic dream of no value and reality. The only thing important here is we are now starting to remember the truth of our eternal existence and Identity when individual reasoning and love are engaged and the false convictions and their respective hypnotic negative experiences are destroyed.[168]

No virtue nor individual lost or left out

Just like all hypnotic dreams, the illusion of finite, material beings containing life and intelligence in a finite, material universe will simply vanish and be forgotten when the individual is awakened to reality.[169] No true idea is lost. Neither is any individual ego or mind lost or left out. All the inharmonious and seemingly significant events in the hypnotic nightmare including crimes against humanity are dissolved and disappear in the appearing reality of the truth. The true Identity, Being and Ego of our most villainous and horrible human characters are as much the one perfect Being as are our most virtuous. Some may simply have more tenacious and erroneous beliefs and convictions to suffer through and eradicate than others, but everyone will eventually make it because all were it to begin with, before their individual nightmare started at their mistakenly believed conception and birth of a false, separate human ego and identity.[170] All lies when believed true by way of identity theft are hypnotic, dreamlike illusions that must be suffered through while the erroneous belief in the lie is uncorrected by intelligent reasoning and therefore will continue to prevail causing continued and repeated sufferings until they are corrected[171] and now, intelligent reasoning in this arena has given us the power and understanding to correct these errors. The nightmarish dream never happened in reality but only in the individual hypnotic dream of an ego that really never was. The one Mind that is truly you, the only Life and individual there is, was never aware of any of it. It wasn't sleeping or unconscious to truth, and does not even know what sleep is. The objective big bang illusion was nothing but a *dead-end*-street. A reversed and upside-down hypnotic dream caused by *individual,* erroneous beliefs of an imagined alien ego. The *individual human ego* will eventually be forced to turn around on its dead-end street and return to reasoning, correct these mistaken convictions and beliefs and thereby remember and live its true Ego and Identity in reality. The one, complete and whole Consciousness can only truly know and be aware of Itself as impersonal, eternal, celestial, infinite, Life, perfection, truth and love everywhere.[172] The various histories of the so-called material big bang universe of hypnotic illusion-ideas, mistakes and lies along with all the suffering, false appetites, superior or inferior complexes, grief, confusion, violence, wars, hate, and revenge we may have mistakenly dreamed as humans was all really for naught and will fade away for it all occurred in an imaginary, hypnotic dream of illusions, never happened and was never known in reality.[173] Clearly, before the unreal, illusory, hypnotic, so-called objective big bang universe that never was, I, the single Intelligence and Ego aware of myself as eternal Life, infinite truth and perfect love - *individually* AM.[174]

The light of the body is the eye: if therefore thine eye be single, thy whole body shall be full of light.

But if thine eye be evil, thy whole body shall be full of darkness. If therefore the light that is in thee be darkness, how great is that darkness!

Matthew 6:22,23

Chapter 7

Application

This chapter is intentionally short and sweet simply because your correct application of the truth and reality to lies and illusions is, well, short and sweet. Through your accurate reasoning and better understanding of your Identity, you find yourself to be the impersonal, conscious awareness of the singular Mind and Principle behind and in which all being and phenomena of the universe resides subjectively as the mental expression of that singular Mind. You reasoned that in reality there could never be a finite, objective, material universe outside of the mental element of consciousness and that this so-called objectivity of space and things in it can only occur in subjective, hypnotic illusions and dreams. These mistaken illusions are just mental illusion-ideas and phenomena within your consciousness and therefore, can be manipulated, controlled and corrected as all erring ideas in mind can. Through further reasoning you find that the actual, real nature of this singular Mind, of this impersonal singularity, is perfect Intelligence. It is the only "thing" there is. Furthermore, it is the only Ego and is consciously aware of itself *individually* as the only individual and the only Identity, presence, Life and power there is, which in its whole and complete entirety, is the universe and is you. You always were and always will be manifested as the infinite, complete and perfect, conscious awareness of your intelligent and forever, impersonal, harmonious self. This accurate awareness of the celestial Self - I AM - is also the correct interpretation, meaning and Identity of everyone, everything, everywhere in the universe. You *are* the universe. This simply means that the presence and meaning of this one Being is everyone, is everywhere and is everything consisting of every idea that is good and perfect. The entire *true* universe is the *individual* Identity and expression of one complete, singular Being and Principle and is one and the same as *your* conscious awareness that is *my* conscious awareness of myself as the *only* whole, perfect and complete presence of ALL - I AM ALL ONE.

Remember, my I is your I in our true Identity. Therefore, *any* inharmonious supposition, suggestion, argument or belief (that must all be hypnotic illusions), while seeming to be coming from your own consciousness (one and the same with your universe) that in any way distorts, reverses, or testifies contrarily to my impersonal and harmonious singularity of Life and Ego, of my Intelligence and perfect condition, presence, power, Life and Identity everywhere, is no longer my true Consciousness but is that of an imagined, separate, alien ego. In its childish nightmare, this imagined, whacked-out ego has nothing else to work with than the facts about me and is simply acknowledging me already there but in an improper and misunderstood manner as if seeing my reality through an out of focus lens distorting my true meanings. My harmonious facts will always be there as the facts always are. They are reality, will always be present and will never be lost. However, when viewed from this separate, imitation ego, my harmonious facts of self and Being will hypnotically appear as reversed, distorted and upside down illusions presenting what now seems to be, a finite, material universe with inharmonious laws and events and a personal *you* as one of many very limited, finite creatures and organic bodies in it. Instead of being one complete, mental, harmonious, eternal Life and universe, you will be a finite, organic speck in an out-of-focus, upside-down, counterfeit, objective universe composed of reversed, finite, incomplete, inharmonious hypnotic lies, illusions and death.

Unreal and inharmonious lies and illusions, in an *infinity* of my harmonious facts and reality, can never be real but can appear to be real if the illusion-idea they ride on is believed to be true. These illusions are conceived and caused by a mistaken belief of a *separate,* make-believe mind that could never exist or think *separately* from my Mind but only seems to hypnotically in its imagination just like any dream does. As has been reasoned, there is just my one, infinite and singular Identity, known to myself as I AM, the only thinking mechanism, the only cause and effect in existence. I AM the only Identity in existence and my intelligent Identity simultaneously contains and is all attributes of an infinite perfect universe of expressed intelligence. We, you, me, us - are all I AM - the one singularity that is always impersonal, infinite, perfect and good. Infinite individual awareness of my individual self, of this singular Life, of my perfect attributes and Identity that is everyone, everywhere and everything - is the only idea and effect in existence. *I AM THE ONLY TRUTH AND THE ONLY REALITY.* Therefore, in the infinity where only my one Being and self exists and is all, where only my perfect, thinking, intelligent cause and *individual* awareness of my infinite self has always existed in reality as I AM, the mistaken belief of an additional and separate, thinking ego as *another* creator, as *another* being, as *another* self, as *another* identity, as *another* i am arising in the arrogant individual mentality is a colossal illusion and mistake. Cause and its effect are always one. Likewise the mind and its universe are always one. Projected forth as either the effect of the true Mind or the false, separate mind - your expression of *you* is always the universe revealed to you. Accordingly, the distorted consequences of this mistaken "whacked-out" erring mentality believing itself to be a separate thinking cause will be grim illusions indeed. Not seeing and understanding my reality or my true Identity properly, the mistaken individual's new self and new identity residing in its newly generated hypnotic illusion will now believe this illusion to be real and the only. Most importantly—the alien ego is claiming and you are believing this self—to be YOU! Thrust outside of my reality due to its own selfish desire to be separate, out of my conscious awareness of my true self, this so-called *separate* mind and identity will now cause an array of *separate* effects that can never be original ideas and conditions as these require my genuine Intelligence and Life to be truly facts. Outside of my reality and with no ideas of its own to work with, this whacked-out and imagined non-mind alien can only bring forth and experience reversals, illusions and counterfeits of my true ideas - reality. Logically, these illusions must be unreal, imperfect, and nightmarish as all distortions and lies of my true, harmonious facts and ideas must always be.

As we have reasoned, there cannot be multiple, objective, and finite people, places, things, and inharmonious conditions in reality but only as distorted illusions likened to watching a movie that is being projected through a grossly out of focus lens. All those objective people, places, things, and inharmonious conditions are really my one, harmonious self that was always there enjoying the warmth of my whole, infinite, *individuality, and perfect attributes* but are being temporarily viewed through the distorted lens of imagined, whacked-out minds claiming to be separate identities out in the cold, dead realm of their own selfish illusions and dreams. My reality, power, and truth were always there and will always be available to enjoy if only it was understood how to get that pesky lens in our projector analogy back in focus.

Seeing my reality hypnotically and erroneously projected through the out of focus lens caused by this new and separate self through identity theft, this imagined, alien ego observes the following distortions and false illusions: First and foremost instead of my reality, it will have unreality; instead of the eternal, timeless I AM, my impersonal, infinite Being and Ego, it will now be many limited egos with brief birth-life-death cycles claiming "i am". Instead of Living and being aware of my truth, these separate egos will be dead to my reality. Instead of timeless facts, it will always present lies and illusions with a finite timeline, that is, unreal illusions will have a start, a life, and an end. They will be dying in their own illusions that deny them a true sense and awareness of my perfect singularity and eternal Life presence. Instead of being aware of my infinite, *individual* self and Identity - I AM - *as* the entire and *only* universe, it will be aware of its individual self and identity *as* a very limited form that, for the believed-to-be-human being is the diminutive and personal meat-sack container living as a tiny, organic and vulnerable speck in an immense objective universe. Instead of the only substance solely being my ideas and my presence, it will believe its life lives in and is dependent upon many material substances that are also hypnotic illusions that don't even exist. Instead of a good and perfect quality everywhere in my body of awareness that is the only universe, it will experience imperfect qualities in a limited and finite life that eventually seems to end in *another* death - right within its unbeknownst present death that all so-called "living" creatures are when *outside* my true Life. Without sound reasoning that exposes these lies and hypnotic illusions for what they truly are, where they came from, why they are projected erroneously and how to destroy them, this so-called separated mind and ego believes in and is now "stuck" with all these hypnotic disasters as true, factual experiences as it blindly and sadly marches through "time" to another "fact" of its so-called "life" - its inevitable death. A death that it was all along while mistakenly believing to be true Life that only I possess.

Through fear and/or intimidation of the separate mind from not knowing the truth that my one, perfect, impersonal Identity and infinite individuality is the only reality - all else contrary to my reality are simply hypnotic illusions. Starting with the imagined, separate mind that generated them, the illusion unfolds as a false and imagined sense of *you* and others as separated, personal beings with material, objective bodies in an objective, inharmonious universe hypnotically appearing on the screen of one's life experience. Through this subtle identity theft of your true Consciousness and Ego that occurred as a result of the alien mind's selfish desire to be separate and distinct, you must now suffer through the very lies and distorted illusions the alien mind has generated for itself in its newly created life and universe. You, now believing your own life, identity and self to be this separated mind, ego and body are now temporarily dead to the harmonious truth, facts, and awareness of Your True Being. Welcome to the human race! - a race lost from the start and going nowhere but in vain circles in its imagined progress and evolution or perhaps "circling the drain" would be more accurate, a phrase used by some in the medical community to describe an inevitable death!

Nature of the hypnotic lies and illusions

Whatever the inharmonious conditions are that seemed to have reversed my harmonious facts pertaining to Life, health, harmony, abundance, peace and happiness, they are all one and the same thing; subjective, hypnotic illusions and lies - never anything real! Hypnotically the imagined, alien ego has reversed and distorted my harmonious facts that were always there and distorted them subjectively on the life screen of a deluded consciousness. Fearful, inharmonious, hypnotic illusions and experiences seek to obscure and steal your true awareness of my perfect, eternal and *only* Being and Life that is actually You, an entirely mental and harmonious "YOU" that was always there as ME and always will be. But the factual awareness of my one, infinite perfect self and Identity has become obscured and diluted by identity theft where an alien mind has projected "being" as an erroneous material, finite, objective universe composed of hypnotic lies and illusions. A so-called physical, objective universe with separate human beings locked in birth-life-death sequences that experience a limited and challenged life as incomplete, personal, separate male and female organic individuals. In this alien life, leading examples of hypnotic lies, illusions and failures are disease, poverty, ignorance and death. Further inharmonious examples in the illusion are failing economies, inept governments, wars, destructive weather, accidents, disasters, substance abuse, inordinate lust, greed, depression, destructive relationships, etc., etc. Generally, anything that suggests negative, erroneous ideas contrary to, reversing and opposing my harmonious and perfect oneness of my infinite Being.

Source of the hypnotic lies and illusions

The one and only source that lies and illusions have in common is that they are *all* the false, hypnotic and inharmonious outcome of the identity theft of you, the awareness of I AM; your whole and complete Ego and Life by the imaginary, insidious, personal, believed-to-be separate, alien and wannabe mind. This so-called additional, thinking creator that claims in its pathetic experience, "i am a separate and distinct ego and life. i am a thinking, creating, human being." This make-believe "i am," that is the mistaken awareness of an imagined, separate, personal human consciousness and ego will always automatically cause discord as both the source and as its own duped believer and victim. Ignorantly it believes all discord and limitations to be real events in its real life and itself to be an actual thinking mind, ego and life; a being outside of and in addition to my only, real, Mind, Ego and Being there is. Claiming and believing to be a *separate*, thinking ego can only manifest *separate* "facts and ideas" in addition to the *only* infinite facts and ideas. These *separate* "facts and ideas" can only be whacked-out, hypnotic *lies and reversals about* my true facts and ideas.

In another analogy, the claim of being a so-called separate, thinking mind will reverse and distort everything and will be like turning a switch from REALITY to unreality. From ETERNAL LIFE to continual death. From PERFECT ONENESS to confused, incomplete and limited many. From HEALTH AND HARMONY to sickness, pain and suffering. From ETERNAL, IMPERSONAL, AND WHOLE CELESTIAL BEING, IDENTITY, AND AWARENESS to a birth-life-death cycle in a pathetic, ignorant and diminutive personal meat-sack human being, identity and awareness.

I, the only perfect thinking entity in existence have already thought of, know and AM aware of myself to be the *only Ego and universe* that is impersonal, non-material, perfect, good *and* infinite. Therefore when another, so-called additional thinking, creating entity seeming to be *outside of my infinite, perfect Being* - a thief ignorantly and arrogantly claiming "i am a separate being, i can think and i can create too," every harmonious fact about my Life and existence will be hypnotically turned upside down, reversed and made troublesome and painful for the imagined, whacked-out, separate, alien ego. Erroneously believing to be an actual thinking, and therefore causing entity outside of my infinite, perfect Intelligence, the only Life, cause, effect and singularity there is, can never happen in reality but can in an unreal dream. In this nightmare the imagined alien ego's so-called thinking, causing and manifesting activities will simply be direct reversals and distortions of my facts rendering them limited, imperfect, inharmonious, and enveloped within a finite timeline. This is due to the *infinite* and timeless nature of the only real Ego there is, Intelligence, whose *man*ifestation and awareness of Itself is the only true *Man*. Infinitely complete, perfect and good, Intelligence can only be experienced *individually* as the singular eternal awareness of I AM ALL ONE.

Destroying the hypnotic lies and illusions reveals my reality

To battle this imagined and albeit aggressively harmful and deadly make-believe mind, thief and creator that now seems to be you on this nightmarish *dead-end* street you call life, only a general method need be presented here because the operating mechanism of *all lies* and illusions share the same common cause - identity theft. By proclaiming the true, harmonious Identity of yourself while reasoning and understanding that there can be no other actual, additional, thinking mind to hypnotically distort the facts, you can *fearlessly* reverse and invalidate the specific lies and illusions. Know and feel, that is, *realize* and become aware that your true Identity is not and can never be an imagined, separate ego subject to the dream of human tribulation. It is always the perfect singularity, the only Mind, Principle, Intelligence and Life there ever was or ever will be. Fearlessly invalidate illusions and their source as unreal, hypnotic out-of-focus distortions, identities and counterfeits. Simultaneously proclaim, know and feel the truth of your Being which will automatically reveal harmony exactly where the seeming reversal of your true State was. There was never anything *really* wrong or distorted! The presence of your perfect Self has always been there and everywhere! The lens of your Life projector is back in focus! The hypnotic illusion of an objective, inharmonious, material universe and a separate, organic being as a tiny personal speck was never something that actually was. It was never conceived of nor thought of, but was simply your truth projected through a temporary out of focus lens from the erring conviction and point of view of an imagined, separate ego. There was never some additional, mysterious force or mind "out there" causing the illusions of finite, material things and wrong conditions that at the time seemed to be real phenomena "outside" of your *infinite,* perfect intelligence. Just your perfect attributes and facts temporarily not being projected, seen and understood correctly by the imagined and deluded alien mind in a dream. Courageously, through careful reasoning invalidate the hypnotic lies and illusions along with that imaginary, so-called separate mind that caused all these inharmonious challenges and limitations, to your harmonious awareness of the truth and oneness of your Being that is I AM. Through repeated reasoning and understanding, fearlessly know and feel that I AM the only individual awareness of the only Self; pure, impersonal, Intelligence. I, *individually,* AM aware of myself as the only Life and only Identity there is, an infinite Being, an infinite Life and an infinite, impersonal, harmonious, celestial individual - I AM infinitely revealed - perfectly - everywhere - eternally NOW!

What was always there is revealed

You, your conscious awareness right now; you, your individuality and Ego right now; you, your Life right now is the one and only, infinite, harmonious Truth - I AM a complete, singular, celestial, impersonal Life. My body is the conscious awareness of myself that is the perfect and harmonious *Identity and meaning* of everyone, everything and everywhere in my universe - always. In seeing and understanding correctly, that is, in *realizing* I AM the true, infinite Ego, the only Identity, the only cause, creator and awareness of myself manifested as the impersonal body of my perfect, subjective universe, I simultaneously understand that there is simply nothing else real going on...*ever*...and that is the short and sweet of it, the truth, love, and fulfillment of my infinite, singular, complete, perfect Life and Identity that is always YOU AND ME AS ONE and always has been. Clearly WE can say *individually and impersonally* as the one and only Identity there is, "Before the identity theft by an imagined, whacked-out, separate ego and its hypnotic illusion and self-expressed image and likeness of organic human beings in a so-called objective, finite, big bang universe that never was, I—THE INFINITE INDIVIDUALITY OF PERFECT LIFE, TRUTH AND LOVE - THE ONLY UNIVERSE THERE IS—AM.

Epilogue

Logically, there can be only one truth about any subject and this holds true for life just as it does for mathematics, physics, music, etc. To study and understand life is identical to studying and understanding consciousness and mind, for they are all one and the same. No longer based on ancient superstitions or on blind, erroneous beliefs and dogma, our common sense reasoning has taken us beyond so-called objective physics and we now find the universe to be a mental, subjective universe of ideas residing in us, in consciousness. This improved understanding enables us to cast out false, malicious, cruel beliefs and their manifestations allowing us to prove and demonstrate that the reasoning and principles employed are sound. As the endnotes indicate, the principles covered in this book coincide with Genesis through Revelation and other texts of the world's major religions because they are all rooted on the same, *non-religious,* intelligent, scientific principle and reasoning; the infinite Oneness of Perfect, Intelligent Being where anything contrary to this eternal perfection are false illusions generated by a separate, alien ego - a liar and a murderer. The prophets, and Jesus in particular who mastered this subject as is proven by his *unparalleled demonstrations,* understood this. You could say Jesus was the world's "Einstein" of metaphysics and *not religion!* These individuals performed these so-called miracles because they understood and applied the principles they intelligently reasoned to be true. These so-called miracles were not miracles at all but were simply the practical, tangible, and proven outcome of the Principles they understood. As we gain a more accurate understanding of these Principles, apply them, and begin to demonstrate and prove them for ourselves, we find we are not in conflict with, nor alienated from those ancient texts, nor from the courageous and wise prophets, those wonderful men and women whose lives inspired those great works. Rather, with increased warmth and clarity, we are now drawn even closer to them and can embrace their teachings as the forever bedrock of our Soul and Universe. These Principles and their illusion-destroying power are what they were attempting to teach and prove to us, not some mysterious religion based on blind faith and illogical beliefs.[175]

I had three compelling reasons for writing this book. First and foremost was to present the harmonious truth and reality of our being and universe in a logical manner using modern language and arguments. Second, to deal with the inharmonious challenges that are nothing but false illusions humans face every day in their so-called physical, objective universe. The perfect and harmonious truth of our being when understood and applied will dramatically reduce the world's suffering whatever that suffering may be including escalating, crippling and obnoxious healthcare costs. Applying the facts instead of mistakes *always* results in harmonious success.

Lastly, this old world needs some *serious* adult supervision! Correctly understanding who we *really are* would be especially useful to world leaders and populations today. Unfortunately, the world's various cultures are mostly based upon misunderstanding our true nature while entertaining mistaken beliefs about religion and reality that has polarized the masses into the idiotic and dangerous "us, them and a separated, personal God" mentality. This mistaken mentality has caused tremendous suffering and death in the past and it seems to be escalating today—all in the name of *emotional and baseless beliefs, both cultural and religious* that actually are, in fact, the irrational and distorted doctrines of an imagined, separate, malevolent, alien ego.

A prime example of how whacked out and dangerous these idiotic beliefs have become, there are many world leaders and large segments of the population today who believe a conflagration in the Middle East will usher in some kind of supernatural intervention on behalf of a select few (on *their* side, of course)! At times it almost seems they are inviting this calamity as a means of escape to find perfection and peace when only bitter disappointment and no peace awaits them![176] Their timing and heartfelt desires are right but they got the wrong war! AGAIN!! Lied to and fooled once more by the malevolent alien! Their so-called Armageddon and Apocalypse are nothing more than a tragic misunderstanding of what is *really* going on right now, in this, the final war in the age of reason (the *real Armageddon!*) and the accompanying unveiling of our True Identity (the *real Apocalypse!*)

It was never "us, them, and a separated, personal God" but was always the infinite singularity and individuality of "I AM", the *only* Life, and the attendant harmony that always follows the realization of true facts versus mistaken beliefs. Death, destruction, and calamities are gateways to nowhere - they are nothing but more disappointing failures presented to us via the one and only source of all lies and illusions - the separate, alien, human ego! A mantra from the 1960s used to say, "Let anyone believe or do whatever they want as long as they don't harm anyone else"... well, that's fine but these misled children of the world are playing with matches and *they will* burn the house down to the ground unless some rational thought and adult supervision inter-venes.[177] This book, *Satan's Looming Identity Crisis! The Final War in the Age of Reason* is one of the many rational explanations and serious "adult supervisors" our illusion so desperately needs at this crucial time.

In writing this book, I have not set out to destroy anything real - only false beliefs and illusions that seek to harm and imprison us are in danger of being destroyed; the freeing truth and perfect reality of Being are never in danger of being destroyed. I have only set out to reinstate the truth of our nature that our prophets were trying to teach us in the first place. Life has always been a logical science with fixed, intelligent principles and laws just like mathematics, music, physics, etc. Today we take much pride in how technologically advanced our civilization has become through our intelligent reasoning ability where we have mas-tered these many disciplines. We have made it up to the mouth of the cave. It is time to extend that same intelligent reasoning to *all* aspects of our experience, leave this cave of lies and illusions, this womb and tomb of ignorance and death and find our *only* True Life and Identity - the Infinite, Harmonious and Singular Mind of Perfect, Eternal Being.

I,

INTELLIGENCE,

AM

THE ONE AND ONLY LIFE,

THE ONE AND ONLY UNIVERSE,

WHOLLY IMPERSONAL AND PERFECT,

WITHOUT A BEGINNING AND WITHOUT

THE END

Bibliography

Holy Bible. Authorized King James Version

The Gnostic Bible, Gnostic Texts of Mystical Wisdom from the Ancient and Medieval Worlds-Pagan, Jewish, Christian, Mandaean, Islamic, and Cathar. Edited by Willis Barnstone and Marvin Meyer, Boston & London, Shambhala Publications, Inc., 2003

Eddy, Mary Baker. *Prose Works other than Science and Health.* Boston, Massachusetts, Published by the First Church of Christ, Scientist, 1953

Eddy, Mary Baker. *Science and Health with Key to the Scriptures.* Boston, Massachusetts, Published by the First Church of Christ, Scientist, 1971

Eustace, Herbert W. *Christian Science Its "Clear and Correct Teaching" and Complete Writings.* Berkeley, California, Lederer, Street and Zeus Co., 1964

Glover, Mary Baker. *Science and Health.* Boston, Christian Science Publishing Company, 1875, reprinted by the Rare Book Company, Freehold, N.J.

Hartmann, W. K., R.J. Phillips, and G.J. Taylor, eds. 1986. <u>Origin of the Moon</u>. (Houston: Lunar and Planetary Institute.)

Kappeler, Max. *The Science of the Oneness of Being in the Christian Science Textbook*. Wilmington, Delaware, Kappeler Institute Publishing, 1983

Kimball, Edward A. *Teaching and Addresses on Christian Science*. Edited by Rev. G. A. Kratzer, Santa Clarita, California, The Bookmark

Nowell, Ames, C.S.B., D.D., Th.D. *Mary Baker Eddy, Her Revelation of Divine Egoism*. Veritas Institute, Inc., 1965, reprinted by the Rare Book Company, Freehold, N.J.

Pagels, Elaine *The Gnostic Gospels*, New York, New York, Published by Random House, 1979

Walter, William W. *The Sickle*. Pacific Palisades, California, William W. Walter trust, 1946

Walter, William W. *The Sharp Sickle*. London, U.K., William W. Walter, 1938

Wright, Helen M. *Made Whole Through Our Marriage to God*. Poulsbo, Washington, Helen M. Wright Pub. Inc., 1996

ENDNOTES

[1] Bede's Library, *The Myth of the Flat Earth*.

[2] Ptolemy of Alexandria, Egypt, *Almagest* (2nd century AD).

[3] Nicolaus Copernicus, *De Revolutionibus* (1543).

[4] Maurice A. Finocchiaro, *The Galileo Affair: A Documentary History* (University of California Press, 1989).

[5] Proverbs 4:5-8
[5] Get wisdom, get understanding: forget it not; neither decline from the words of my mouth.
[6] Forsake her not, and she shall preserve thee: love her, and she shall keep thee.
[7] Wisdom is the principal thing; therefore get wisdom: and with all thy getting get understanding.
[8] Exalt her, and she shall promote thee: she shall bring thee to honour, when thou dost embrace her.

[6] John 8:32
[32] And ye shall know the truth, and the truth shall make you free.

[7] Genesis 3:17(excerpt)
(The verse below states, "cursed is the ground for thy sake". The unpleasant nature of cursed conditions will eventually lead us to discover

why the ground is cursed, enabling us to eliminate the cause of these undesirable conditions.)

[17] And unto Adam he said, Because thou hast hearkened unto the voice of thy wife, and hast eaten of the tree, of which I commanded thee, saying, Thou shalt not eat of it: cursed is the ground for thy sake....

[8] Colossians 1:16,17

[16] For by him were all things created, that are in heaven, and that are in Earth, visible and invisible, whether they be thrones, or dominions, or principalities, or powers: all things were created by him, and for him:

[17] And he is before all things, and by him all things consist.

[9] *The Gnostic Bible,* edited by Willis Barnstone and Marvin Myer (Shambhala Publications, Inc., 2003).

In The Gospel of Mary, first chapter, entitled, "Students Speak with the Savior":

> "Will matter be destroyed or not?" The savior said, "All natures, all formed things, all creatures exist in and with one another and will be resolved into their own roots. The nature of matter is resolved into its nature alone. Whoever has ears to hear should hear."

[10] Psalms 139:7-12

(Below, "spirit" is taken to mean consciousness, mind, ego, mentality, life, etc.)

[7] Whither shall I go from thy spirit? or whither shall I flee from thy presence?

[8] If I ascend up into heaven, thou art there: if I make my bed in hell, behold, thou art there.

[9] If I take the wings of the morning, and dwell in the uttermost parts of the sea;

[10] Even there shall thy hand lead me, and thy right hand shall hold me.

[11] If I say, Surely the darkness shall cover me; even the night shall be light about me.

[12] Yea, the darkness hideth not from thee; but the night shineth as the day: the darkness and the light are both alike to thee.

[11] Genesis 3:7
(Vulnerability is now sensed when their eyes were opened and they knew they were naked and needed protection in aprons.)
[7] And the eyes of them both were opened, and they knew that they were naked; and they sewed fig leaves together, and made themselves aprons.

[12] 1 John 4:18
[18] There is no fear in love; but perfect love casteth out fear: because fear hath torment. He that feareth is not made perfect in love.

[13] Acts 17:27-28
[27] That they should seek the Lord, if haply they might feel after him, and find him, though he be not far from every one of us:
[28] For in him we live, and move, and have our being; as certain also of your own poets have said, For we are also his offspring.

[14] Mark 16:17-18, John 14:12
[17] And these signs shall follow them that believe; In my name shall they cast out devils; they shall speak with new tongues;
[18] They shall take up serpents; and if they drink any deadly thing, it shall not hurt them; they shall lay hands on the sick, and they shall recover.

[12] Verily, verily, I say unto you, He that believeth on me, the works that I do shall he do also; and greater works than these shall he do; because I go unto my Father.

[15] Deuteronomy 4:35
(Below, the names LORD and God were used to name this infinite consciousness.)
[35] Unto thee it was shewed, that thou mightest know that the LORD he is God; there is none else beside him.

[16] 2 Corinthians 3:5
("God" here is taken to mean Consciousness or Intelligence the only entity where true conscious awareness, activity, thinking, knowing and feeling can occur.)
[5] Not that we are sufficient of ourselves to think any thing as of ourselves; but our sufficiency is of God;

¹⁷ John 5:30-31

(Again, "Father" here is taken to mean Consciousness or Intelligence, the only entity where conscious awareness, mental activity, thinking, knowing and feeling can occur and not in an erring belief of a human "self," mind or ego where "my witness is not true.")

[**30**] I can of mine own self do nothing: as I hear, I judge: and my judgment is just; because I seek not mine own will, but the will of the Father which hath sent me.

[**31**] If I bear witness of myself, my witness is not true.

¹⁸ Matthew 19:17

[**17**] And he said unto him, Why callest thou me good? There is none good but one, that is, God: but if thou wilt enter into life, keep the commandments.

¹⁹ John 15:26,27

[**26**] But when the Comforter is come, whom I will send unto you from the Father, even the Spirit of truth, which proceedeth from the Father, he shall testify of me:

[**27**] And ye also shall bear witness, because ye have been with me from the beginning.

²⁰ John 10:30

(As indicated by the word *"my"* in italics, this word was not in the original Greek text. Again, the word "Father" is the term used then for Infinite Intelligence, the sole cause of all reality. All consciousness can only be one entity.)

[**30**] I and *my* Father are one.

²¹ John 14:12 (partial)

("Believeth on me" is nonsensical if it means to blindly believe in the man Jesus. That would be like a math teacher telling students that by simply believing in him, they could go out and work math problems correctly. Clearly "believeth on me" means to understand what Jesus was teaching and then he will be able to demonstrate those same works and even greater works than these.)

[**12**] Verily, verily, I say unto you, He that believeth on me, the works that I do shall he do also; and greater works than these shall he do;

[22] John 1:3
(Clearly in this passage, reality is created/revealed by Intelligence, "All things were made by him…," but the illusion of objective materiality is understood to be nothing but unreal, hypnotic, dreamlike phenomena, "…and without him was not any thing made that was made"!)
[**3**] All things were made by him; and without him was not any thing made that was made.

[23] Matthew 26:26
(The bread, of course, is the Truth, the real "food" of Life or "body" of understanding that Jesus was attempting to explain to the disciples as he "blessed it, brake it" and asked them to "eat" it.)
[**26**] And as they were eating, Jesus took bread, and blessed it, and brake it, and gave it to the disciples, and said, Take, eat; this is my body.

[24] Exodus 3:14
[**14**] And God said unto Moses, I AM THAT I AM: and he said, Thus shalt thou say unto the children of Israel, I AM hath sent me unto you.

[25] John 10:30 & Revelation 1:8
(Again it is noted in verse John 10:30 below, that the word "*my*" is italicized, indicating it was not in the original Greek text and was later added. In essence, the verse is indicating that "I," the only cause, is infinite Intelligence or the "Father." The Self awareness or reflection of this infinite "I" is consciously known as "AM" or the Son in the Father/Son or cause/effect relationship and is always preserved. Of course, verse Revelation 1:8 below is another way of saying, "I AM ALL." Always was, always will be one, infinite, omnipotent, Being. No conscious element or idea can reside outside of the all powerful and infinite ALL, "…the Almighty"!!!!)
[**30**] I and *my* Father are one.

[**8**] I am Alpha and Omega, the beginning and the ending, saith the Lord, which is, and which was, and which is to come, the Almighty.

[26] Genesis 2:6-7, 3:22,23, 1:26,27
(The confused, erring belief that we—that is, our conscious egos—are separated from the only Ego and somehow live in and are dependent on a material body is indeed a mystery and is expressed as "But there went up a mist from the Earth." Verse 7 below describes the erroneous belief commonly held by humans where the false effect, man the human

being, becomes the cause, a living soul. He is now dependent on the dust and air in his nostrils for life.

Whereas the true man, the true <u>man</u>ifestation or reflection of Intelligence, was already present and described as the "image and likeness" of Spirit or Intelligence in Genesis 1:26,27 cited below and prior to the appearance of the "man of the dust." The image and likeness of a spiritual or a mental entity, Intelligence, can never be dust of the ground or finite, limited, matter that are all finite, illusion-ideas.

Verse [7], [22] and [23] below are describing the entire illusion-idea supported by the belief humans have of "self" and "reality," the erring location of man's consciousness and the consequences of this error (LORD God sent him forth from the garden of Eden). The <u>life-less</u> illusion-idea, a so-called physical <u>man</u>ifestation or man becoming consciousness, a living, thinking soul is impossible except in an erroneous, hypnotic dream state and is mocked in, "Behold, the man (a lifeless illusion-idea) is become as one of us (consciousness), to know good and evil.")

Genesis 2:6,7

[6] But there went up a mist from the Earth, and watered the whole face of the ground.

[7] And the LORD God formed man of the dust of the ground, and breathed into his nostrils the breath of life; and man became a living soul.

Genesis 1:26,27

[26] And God said, Let us make man in our image, after our likeness: and let them have dominion over the fish of the sea, and over the fowl of the air, and over the cattle, and over all the Earth, and over every creeping thing that creepeth upon the Earth.

[27] So God created man in his own image, in the image of God created he him; male and female created he them.

Genesis 3:22,23

[22] And the LORD God said, Behold, the man is become as one of us, to know good and evil: and now, lest he put forth his hand, and take also of the tree of life, and eat, and live for ever:

[23] Therefore the LORD God sent him forth from the garden of Eden, to till the ground from whence he was taken.

---

[27] Romans 1:23, 25

[23] And changed the glory of the uncorruptible God into an image made like to corruptible man, and to birds, and four-footed beasts, and creeping things.

[**25**] Who changed the truth of God into a lie, and worshipped and served the creature more than the Creator, who is blessed for ever. Amen.

²⁸ I Corinthians 12:12-20
("Christ" is taken to mean the conscious awareness of the ideas that identify the infinite *Individuality* of infinite Intelligence or "Spirit," and is the impersonal "body of understanding" of the Truth. Christ is the "AM," the effect, <u>mani</u>festation or Son of "I," where the "I," the Father is infinite, perfect Intelligence and is the sole cause of this self aware-ness or reflection. Like the infinite number of rays carrying the identity and all the details of one entity, the sun, so too there exists an infinite number of impersonal individuals enjoying their identity as the one perfect Soul or Ego.)

[**12**] For as the body is one, and hath many members, and all the mem-bers of that one body, being many, are one body: so also is Christ.

[**13**] For by one Spirit are we all baptized into one body, whether we be Jews or Gentiles, whether we be bond or free; and have been all made to drink into one Spirit.

[**14**] For the body is not one member, but many.

[**15**] If the foot shall say, Because I am not the hand, I am not of the body; is it therefore not of the body?

[**16**] And if the ear shall say, Because I am not the eye, I am not of the body; is it therefore not of the body?

[**17**] If the whole body were an eye, where were the hearing? If the whole were hearing, where were the smelling?

[**18**] But now hath God set the members every one of them in the body, as it hath pleased him.

[**19**] And if they were all one member, where were the body?

[**20**] But now are they many members, yet but one body.

²⁹ Romans 1:20
[**20**] For the invisible things of him from the creation of the world are clearly seen, being understood by the things that are made, even his eternal power and Godhead; so that they are without excuse:

³⁰ Colossians 3:10-11
[**10**] And have put on the new man, which is renewed in knowledge after the image of him that created him:

[11] Where there is neither Greek nor Jew, circumcision nor uncircumcision, Barbarian, Scythian, bond nor free: but Christ is all, and in all.

31 *The Gnostic Bible,* edited by Willis Barnstone and Marvin Myer (Shambhala Publications, Inc., 2003) Literature of Gnostic Wisdom, *The Gospel of Truth,* page 247, second paragraph:

> The Father opens his bosom, but his bosom is the Holy Spirit. He reveals his hidden self which is his son, so that through the compassion of the Father the Aeons may know him, end their wearying search for the Father and rest themselves in him, knowing that this is rest. After he had filled what was incomplete, he did away with form. The form of it is the world, that which it served. For where there is envy and strife, there is an incompleteness; but where there is unity, there is completeness. Since this incompleteness came about because they did not know the Father, so when they know the Father, incompleteness, from that moment on, will cease to exist. As one's ignorance disappears when he gains knowledge, and as darkness disappears when light appears, so also incompleteness is eliminated by completeness. Certainly, from that moment on, form is no longer manifest, but will be dissolved in fusion with unity. For now their works lie scattered. In time unity will make the spaces complete. By means of unity each one will understand itself. By means of knowledge it will purify itself of diversity with a view towards unity, devouring matter within itself like fire and darkness by light, death by life.

32 Romans 8:21-23, 38,39

[21] Because the creature itself also shall be delivered from the bondage of corruption into the glorious liberty of the children of God.

[22] For we know that the whole creation groaneth and travaileth in pain together until now.

[23] And not only they, but ourselves also, which have the first fruits of the Spirit, even we ourselves groan within ourselves, waiting for the adoption, to wit, the redemption of our body.

[38] For I am persuaded, that neither death, nor life, nor angels, nor principalities, nor powers, nor things present, nor things to come,

[39] Nor height, nor depth, nor any other creature, shall be able to separate us from the love of God, which is in Christ Jesus our Lord.

33 John 4:21-24
(Again, "Spirit," "God," and "Father" are collectively taken to mean Intelligence, Mind, Ego, Mentality, Life, etc.)
[21] Jesus saith unto her, Woman, believe me, the hour cometh, when ye shall neither in this mountain, nor yet at Jerusalem, worship the Father.
[22] Ye worship ye know not what: we know what we worship: for salvation is of the Jews.
[23] But the hour cometh, and now is, when the true worshippers shall worship the Father in spirit and in truth: for the Father seeketh such to worship him.
[24] God is a Spirit: and they that worship him must worship him in spirit and in truth.

34 John 17:21-23, Isaiah 2:22
(Here Jesus is focused on the whole and perfect singularity of Being, the oneness of reality.)
[21] That they all may be one; as thou, Father, art in me, and I in thee, that they also may be one in us: that the world may believe that thou hast sent me.
[22] And the glory which thou gavest me I have given them; that they may be one, even as we are one:
[23] I in them, and thou in me, that they may be made perfect in one; and that the world may know that thou hast sent me, and hast loved them, as thou hast loved me.

[22] Cease ye from man, whose breath is in his nostrils: for wherein is he to be accounted of?

35 Genesis 2:1-3
[1] Thus the heavens and the Earth were finished, and all the host of them.
[2] And on the seventh day God ended his work which he had made; and he rested on the seventh day from all his work which he had made.
[3] And God blessed the seventh day, and sanctified it: because that in it he had rested from all his work which God created and made.

36 Revelation 22:13
[13] I am Alpha and Omega, the beginning and the end, the first and the last.

³⁷ Mark 12:23-25

(The term "dead," in verse 25 below, is taken to mean believing to be a finite, material human being that understands nothing about and is dead to the true state of Being. Because Jesus knew that organic, material death is not real, his use of the word "dead" meant being dead to the truth. In this light, "rise from the dead" means gaining an understanding of the true state through intelligent reasoning where marriage of separate, dissimilar elements is not applicable in the oneness of Being.)

[**23**] In the resurrection therefore, when they shall rise, whose wife shall she be of them? for the seven had her to wife.

[**24**] And Jesus answering said unto them, Do ye not therefore err, because ye know not the scriptures, neither the power of God?

[**25**] For when they shall rise from the dead, they neither marry, nor are given in marriage; but are as the angels which are in heaven.

³⁸ Colossians 3:3,4, Revelation 21:1-6; 22-25

(Paul, in Colossians 3:3,4 below, is explaining you are dead to true Life when you believe to be a separate human being whereas your true Life is Christ, the singular, manifestation or image and likeness of the one, perfect Intelligence, God. Your true sense of Life is temporarily hidden by the false and dead human sense of separateness, but will reappear when the human sense is discarded.)

[**3**] For ye are dead, and your life is hid with Christ in God.

[**4**] When Christ, who is our life, shall appear, then shall ye also appear with him in glory.

[**1**] And I saw a new heaven and a new Earth: for the first heaven and the first Earth were passed away; and there was no more sea.

[**2**] And I John saw the holy city, new Jerusalem, coming down from God out of heaven, prepared as a bride adorned for her husband.

[**3**] And I heard a great voice out of heaven saying, Behold, the tabernacle of God is with men, and he will dwell with them, and they shall be his people, and God himself shall be with them, and be their God.

[**4**] And God shall wipe away all tears from their eyes; and there shall be no more death, neither sorrow, nor crying, neither shall there be any more pain: for the former things are passed away.

[**5**] And he that sat upon the throne said, Behold, I make all things new. And he said unto me, Write: for these words are true and faithful.

[6] And he said unto me, It is done. I am Alpha and Omega, the beginning and the end. I will give unto him that is athirst of the fountain of the water of life freely.

[22] And I saw no temple therein: for the Lord God Almighty and the Lamb are the temple of it.
[23] And the city had no need of the sun, neither of the moon, to shine in it: for the glory of God did lighten it, and the Lamb is the light thereof.
[24] And the nations of them which are saved shall walk in the light of it: and the kings of the Earth do bring their glory and honour into it.
[25] And the gates of it shall not be shut at all by day: for there shall be no night there.

[39] Hebrews 7:3
[3] Without father, without mother, without descent, having neither beginning of days, nor end of life; but made like unto the Son of God;

[40] Revelation 2:11 & 21:8
(Note the second death in the verses below. The first death occurs at the false belief of "self" consisting of a separate, ego that is manifested and shown forth as a human birth. The individual is now dead to the truth of its true nature and identity. In this human nightmare and illusion, the looming threat of death believed true will <u>always</u> be the second death and can be repeated *ad infinitum* if what caused this frightful, phantom, illusion is not understood and corrected by the individual.)
[11] He that hath an ear, let him hear what the Spirit saith unto the churches; He that overcometh shall not be hurt of the second death.

[8] But the fearful, and unbelieving, and the abominable, and murderers, and whoremongers, and sorcerers, and idolaters, and all liars, shall have their part in the lake which burneth with fire and brimstone: which is the second death.

[41] Luke 23:26-29
(On his way to his crucifixion, Jesus admonishes those who are weeping for him to instead weep for themselves and their children and says those who never bore children are blessed.)
[26] And as they led him away, they laid hold upon one Simon, a Cyrenian, coming out of the country, and on him they laid the cross, that he might bear it after Jesus.

[27] And there followed him a great company of people, and of women, which also bewailed and lamented him.

[28] But Jesus turning unto them said, Daughters of Jerusalem, weep not for me, but weep for yourselves, and for your children.

[29] For, behold, the days are coming, in the which they shall say, Blessed are the barren, and the wombs that never bare, and the paps which never gave suck.

42 John 14:6

[6] Jesus saith unto him, I am the way, the truth, and the life: no man cometh unto the Father, but by me.

(Obviously, in the verse above Jesus is not talking about the man Jesus as "the way, the truth, and the life," but about individual understanding of what he is laboring to teach, the true facts and Identity of the One, Sole, Impersonal, Celestial, Intelligence, Life and Ego ("the Father"), the "I" aware of Itself as the Christ, the Son, the "AM." This "I AM" is the only Life there is and the one we seemed to have died away from when believing to be separate human minds and egos. The so-called objective man Jesus was just the illusion-idea of a human being just like you and I are prior to waking through understanding from the false belief of a separate, material, personal, finite, human existence.)

43 Genesis 2:17

(The awareness of the knowledge of good is knowing the truth of the one, infinite, celestial Ego that we all are as one Being. The knowing of evil is the arrogant and ignorant belief that a separate consciousness or ego is possible as in the disastrous separate ego of the human mind. This erring belief is fiction, a lie, is not the truth and so naturally, must die and cease to be entertained.)

[17] But of the tree of the knowledge of good and evil, thou shalt not eat of it: for in the day that thou eatest thereof thou shalt surely die.

44 John 6:63

[63] It is the spirit that quickeneth; the flesh profiteth nothing: the words that I speak unto you, they are spirit, and they are life.

45 Mark 12:27

[27] He is not the God of the dead, but the God of the living: ye therefore do greatly err.

⁴⁶ John 20:23
(Jesus, after passing through and understanding the illusion of his own "death experience," instructs his disciples that whatever erring convictions and beliefs are held to be true before your "death experience", they will still be there after it.)
[23] Whose soever sins ye remit, they are remitted unto them; and whose soever sins ye retain, they are retained.

⁴⁷ 2 Corinthians 12:9,10 (excerpt)
(Infirmities (failures) when their cause is unraveled, point the way to greater understanding.)
[9] And he said unto me, My grace is sufficient for thee: for my strength is made perfect in weakness. Most gladly therefore will I rather glory in my infirmities, that the power of Christ may rest upon me.
[10] Therefore I take pleasure in infirmities....

⁴⁸ Revelation 21:6-8
[6] And he said unto me, It is done. I am Alpha and Omega, the beginning and the end. I will give unto him that is athirst of the fountain of the water of life freely.
[7] He that overcometh shall inherit all things; and I will be his God, and he shall be my son.
[8] But the fearful, and unbelieving, and the abominable, and murderers, and whoremongers, and sorcerers, and idolaters, and all liars, shall have their part in the lake which burneth with fire and brimstone: which is the second death.

⁴⁹ Luke 15:11-24
[11] And he said, A certain man had two sons:
[12] And the younger of them said to his father, Father, give me the portion of goods that falleth to me. And he divided unto them his living.
[13] And not many days after the younger son gathered all together, and took his journey into a far country, and there wasted his substance with riotous living.
[14] And when he had spent all, there arose a mighty famine in that land; and he began to be in want.
[15] And he went and joined himself to a citizen of that country; and he sent him into his fields to feed swine.
[16] And he would fain have filled his belly with the husks that the swine did eat: and no man gave unto him.

[17] And when he came to himself, he said, How many hired servants of my father's have bread enough and to spare, and I perish with hunger!

[18] I will arise and go to my father, and will say unto him, Father, I have sinned against heaven, and before thee,

[19] And am no more worthy to be called thy son: make me as one of thy hired servants.

[20] And he arose, and came to his father. But when he was yet a great way off, his father saw him, and had compassion, and ran, and fell on his neck, and kissed him.

[21] And the son said unto him, Father, I have sinned against heaven, and in thy sight, and am no more worthy to be called thy son.

[22] But the father said to his servants, Bring forth the best robe, and put it on him; and put a ring on his hand, and shoes on his feet:

[23] And bring hither the fatted calf, and kill it; and let us eat, and be merry:

[24] For this my son was dead, and is alive again; he was lost, and is found. And they began to be merry.

[50] Luke 12:4,5

[4] And I say unto you my friends, Be not afraid of them that kill the body, and after that have no more that they can do.

[5] But I will forewarn you whom ye shall fear: Fear him, which after he hath killed hath power to cast into hell; yea, I say unto you, Fear him.

[51] Revelation 21:6-8

[6] And he said unto me, It is done. I am Alpha and Omega, the beginning and the end. I will give unto him that is athirst of the fountain of the water of life freely.

[7] He that overcometh shall inherit all things; and I will be his God, and he shall be my son.

[8] But the fearful, and unbelieving, and the abominable, and murderers, and whoremongers, and sorcerers, and idolaters, and all liars, shall have their part in the lake which burneth with fire and brimstone: which is the second death.

[52] Genesis 3:1-5, Matthew 8:21-22, Mark 12:27, Colossians 3:3,4

[1] Now the serpent was more subtil than any beast of the field which the LORD God had made. And he said unto the woman, Yea, hath God said, Ye shall not eat of every tree of the garden?

[2] And the woman said unto the serpent, We may eat of the fruit of the trees of the garden:

[3] But of the fruit of the tree which is in the midst of the garden, God hath said, Ye shall not eat of it, neither shall ye touch it, lest ye die.

[4] And the serpent said unto the woman, Ye shall not surely die:

[5] For God doth know that in the day ye eat thereof, then your eyes shall be opened, and ye shall be as gods, knowing good and evil.

[21] And another of his disciples said unto him, Lord, suffer me first to go and bury my father.

[22] But Jesus said unto him, Follow me; and let the dead bury their dead.

[27] He is not the God of the dead, but the God of the living: ye therefore do greatly err.

[3] For ye are dead, and your life is hid with Christ in God.

[4] When Christ, who is our life, shall appear, then shall ye also appear with him in glory.

[53] John 8:51

[51] Verily, verily, I say unto you, If a man keep my saying, he shall never see death.

[54] Romans 1:20

[20] For the invisible things of him from the creation of the world are clearly seen, being understood by the things that are made, even his eternal power and Godhead; so that they are without excuse:

[55] Revelation 22:13

[13] I am Alpha and Omega, the beginning and the end, the first and the last.

[56] John 15:27

[27] And ye also shall bear witness, because ye have been with me from the beginning.

57 Luke 17:20,21

[20] And when he was demanded of the Pharisees, when the kingdom of God should come, he answered them and said, The kingdom of God cometh not with observation:

[21] Neither shall they say, Lo here! or, lo there! for, behold, the kingdom of God is within you.

58 John 8:47-58

[47] He that is of God heareth God's words: ye therefore hear them not, because ye are not of God.

[48] Then answered the Jews, and said unto him, Say we not well that thou art a Samaritan, and hast a devil?

[49] Jesus answered, I have not a devil; but I honour my Father, and ye do dishonour me.

[50] And I seek not mine own glory: there is one that seeketh and judgeth.

[51] Verily, verily, I say unto you, If a man keep my saying, he shall never see death.

[52] Then said the Jews unto him, Now we know that thou hast a devil. Abraham is dead, and the prophets; and thou sayest, If a man keep my saying, he shall never taste of death.

[53] Art thou greater than our father Abraham, which is dead? and the prophets are dead: whom makest thou thyself?

[54] Jesus answered, If I honour myself, my honour is nothing: it is my Father that honoureth me; of whom ye say, that he is your God:

[55] Yet ye have not known him; but I know him: and if I should say, I know him not, I shall be a liar like unto you: but I know him, and keep his saying.

[56] Your father Abraham rejoiced to see my day: and he saw it, and was glad.

[57] Then said the Jews unto him, Thou art not yet fifty years old, and hast thou seen Abraham?

[58] Jesus said unto them, Verily, verily, I say unto you, Before Abraham was, I am.

59 1 John 4:16-18

[16] And we have known and believed the love that God hath to us. God is love; and he that dwelleth in love dwelleth in God, and God in him.

[17] Herein is our love made perfect, that we may have boldness in the day of judgment: because as he is, so are we in this world.

[**18**] There is no fear in love; but perfect love casteth out fear: because fear hath torment. He that feareth is not made perfect in love.

[60] Exodus 20:3, John 1:1-5
[**3**] Thou shalt have no other gods before me.

[**1**] In the beginning was the Word, and the Word was with God, and the Word was God.
[**2**] The same was in the beginning with God.
[**3**] All things were made by him; and without him was not any thing made that was made.
[**4**] In him was life; and the life was the light of men.
[**5**] And the light shineth in darkness; and the darkness comprehended it not.

[61] John 1:3
[**3**] All things were made by him; and without him was not any thing made that was made.

[62] John 7:24, Acts 17:28
[**24**] Judge not according to the appearance, but judge righteous judgment.

[**28**] For in him we live, and move, and have our being; as certain also of your own poets have said, For we are also his offspring.

[63] In *The Holy Bible* (KJV), this so-called creator is called Satan, Devil, liar, father of lies, great dragon, old serpent, and prince of darkness.

Various names for the creator of the so-called physical universe in Gnostic texts are azazi'il, demiurge, nebroel, nimrod, prince of darkness, ptahil, sakla, samael, satanas, and yaldabaoth.

[64] *The Gnostic Bible,* Islamic Literature, *The Mother of Books*, paragraph entitled, Azazi'il and his ranks call God a liar, excerpt, page 701:

"So the cursed Azazi'il, and those who proceeded from his cry fell down from the high king, down into the curtain, and fell for seven thousand years because of seven harsh denials and rejection. These are noted in the Qur'an: denial of the divinity, denial of the kingdom, denial of the glory, denial of the highest god, denial of his godliness, denial of light and denial of the spirit's mind."

65 Deuteronomy 4:35
[**35**] Unto thee it was shewed, that thou mightest know that the LORD he is God; there is none else beside him.

66 Ephesians 2:12, 4:17,18,22,23
[**12**] That at that time ye were without Christ, being aliens from the commonwealth of Israel, and strangers from the covenants of promise, having no hope, and without God in the world:

[**17**] This I say therefore, and testify in the Lord, that ye henceforth walk not as other Gentiles walk, in the vanity of their mind,
[**18**] Having the understanding darkened, being alienated from the life of God through the ignorance that is in them, because of the blindness of their heart:

[**22**] That ye put off concerning the former conversation the old man, which is corrupt according to the deceitful lusts;
[**23**] And be renewed in the spirit of your mind;

67 Isaiah 45:5-7; 47:8-10
(Obviously, "I am the LORD" or "God" in this passage is just general consciousness, still capable of going either way, truth or illusion, fact or fiction, because not only does this passage refer to phenomena of light and peace (only from Intelligence), but also a physical universe and evil, that can only be from the whacked out and opposing mind of the separate, alien ego. Perfect and good Intelligence simply does not and cannot create or even know physical and evil illusions.)
[**5**] I am the LORD, and there is none else, there is no God beside me: I girded thee, though thou hast not known me:
[**6**] That they may know from the rising of the sun, and from the west, that there is none beside me. I am the LORD, and there is none else.
[**7**] I form the light, and create darkness: I make peace, and create evil: I the LORD do all these things.

("I am" in the following passage is again, the separate, alien ego claiming to be the "only". The consequences for this erroneous stance is stated by Intelligence, the only Life and Ego.)

[**8**] Therefore hear now this, thou that art given to pleasures, that dwellest carelessly, that sayest in thine heart, I am, and none else beside me; I shall not sit as a widow, neither shall I know the loss of children:

[9] But these two things shall come to thee in a moment in one day, the loss of children, and widowhood: they shall come upon thee in their perfection for the multitude of thy sorceries, and for the great abundance of thine enchantments.

[10] For thou hast trusted in thy wickedness: thou hast said, None seeth me. Thy wisdom and thy knowledge, it hath perverted thee; and thou hast said in thine heart, I am, and none else beside me.

[68] Revelation 12:3,9

(In verse 9 below, note the word "deceiveth" which must take place for illusions to appear and be believed to be real.)

[3] And there appeared another wonder in heaven; and behold a great red dragon, having seven heads and ten horns, and seven crowns upon his heads.

[9] And the great dragon was cast out, that old serpent, called the Devil, and Satan, which deceiveth the whole world: he was cast out into the Earth, and his angels were cast out with him.

[69] John 8:12

[12] Then spake Jesus again unto them, saying, I am the light of the world: he that followeth me shall not walk in darkness, but shall have the light of life.

[70] Genesis 2:1-3

(Note the word "finished"; not "started" or "this is where the story begins", but finished, done, complete...infinite Intelligence understands and is aware of the infinite ideas it created as itself and may now rest and enjoy these ideas eternally.)

[1] Thus the heavens and the Earth were finished, and all the host of them.

[2] And on the seventh day God ended his work which he had made; and he rested on the seventh day from all his work which he had made.

[3] And God blessed the seventh day, and sanctified it: because that in it he had rested from all his work which God created and made.

[71] 1 John 2:19

[19] They went out from us, but they were not of us; for if they had been of us, they would no doubt have continued with us: but they went out, that they might be made manifest that they were not all of us.

72 Genesis 2:1

[1] Thus the heavens and the Earth were finished, and all the host of them.

73 1 John 2:17-20

[17] And the world passeth away, and the lust thereof: but he that doeth the will of God abideth for ever.

[18] Little children, it is the last time: and as ye have heard that antichrist shall come, even now are there many antichrists; whereby we know that it is the last time.

[19] They went out from us, but they were not of us; for if they had been of us, they would no doubt have continued with us: but they went out, that they might be made manifest that they were not all of us.

[20] But ye have an unction from the Holy One, and ye know all things.

(Christ being the true awareness and Identity of the one harmonious Being, antichrist is the opposing, false identity or anti-truth of this one Being. The "Holy One" is, of course, the whole oneness and reality of the one Being)

74 John 8:44

(In addition to the one Almighty Father that Jesus constantly associates himself with, Jesus now reveals another "father"; the "alien" father that is a liar and the source of all lies.)

[44] Ye are of your father the devil, and the lusts of your father ye will do. He was a murderer from the beginning, and abode not in the truth, because there is no truth in him. When he speaketh a lie, he speaketh of his own: for he is a liar, and the father of it.

75 1 John 2:13-23

(The offspring or Son of Infinite Intelligence can only be its own conscious awareness of the true, factual idea of itself. The Father (cause) is infinite Intelligence and the Son (effect or manifestation) is the conscious awareness or Christ (not the finite Jesus, as this human was temporarily expressed for the sole purpose to communicate to other humans) consisting of Life, Truth and Love, all of which are the idea, identity, reflection and meaning of Intelligence itself - the Father. Antichrist is the mistaken consciousness (offspring) or, a hypnotic awareness and belief of erroneous lies or anti-truths put forth by the imagined, separate, alien ego. Notice the alien ego is described as being separated in the phrase, "They went out from us.")

[13] I write unto you, fathers, because ye have known him that is from the beginning. I write unto you, young men, because ye have overcome the wicked one. I write unto you, little children, because ye have known the Father.

[14] I have written unto you, fathers, because ye have known him that is from the beginning. I have written unto you, young men, because ye are strong, and the word of God abideth in you, and ye have overcome the wicked one.

[15] Love not the world, neither the things that are in the world. If any man love the world, the love of the Father is not in him.

[16] For all that is in the world, the lust of the flesh, and the lust of the eyes, and the pride of life, is not of the Father, but is of the world.

[17] And the world passeth away, and the lust thereof: but he that doeth the will of God abideth for ever.

[18] Little children, it is the last time: and as ye have heard that antichrist shall come, even now are there many antichrists; whereby we know that it is the last time.

[19] They went out from us, but they were not of us; for if they had been of us, they would no doubt have continued with us: but they went out, that they might be made manifest that they were not all of us.

[20] But ye have an unction from the Holy One, and ye know all things.

[21] I have not written unto you because ye know not the truth, but because ye know it, and that no lie is of the truth.

[22] Who is a liar but he that denieth that Jesus is the Christ? He is antichrist, that denieth the Father and the Son.

[23] Whosoever denieth the Son, the same hath not the Father: (but) he that acknowledgeth the Son hath the Father also.

[76] John 8:44
(Again, in addition to the one Almighty Father that Jesus constantly associates himself with, below Jesus reveals another "father," a liar and the source of all lies.)

[44] Ye are of your father the devil, and the lusts of your father ye will do. He was a murderer from the beginning, and abode not in the truth, because there is no truth in him. When he speaketh a lie, he speaketh of his own: for he is a liar, and the father of it.

[77] Genesis 2:4-7
(This second creation, following the one that was announced to be complete and <u>finished</u> in Genesis 2:1-3, is the anti-true, illusion-idea-

universe of the alien ego. In the Bible, the name "God", Intelligence, changes to "LORD God" and is here taken to mean the description of the alien ego's erroneous beliefs that are no longer caused by Intelligence. This alien mind generates the illusion of the heavens and the Earth and the hypnotic illusion of a seeming material universe begins. Here, instead of the true man (the <u>manifestation</u>) in the image and likeness or awareness and consciousness of infinite Intelligence, we have an illusory man (<u>manifestation</u>) in the image and likeness of the separate, finite alien ego. This so-called man is now created out of the dust of the ground or matter, and man, the finite, "material" effect, shadow or illusion-idea is believed to become life itself, a separate and material living soul which is impossible and vulgar. This imagined creation and "life" certainly needed ignorance and mystification to occur, hence "there went up a mist from the Earth" just prior to finite man formed of dust.)

[4] These are the generations of the heavens and of the Earth when they were created, in the day that the LORD God made the Earth and the heavens,

[5] And every plant of the field before it was in the Earth, and every herb of the field before it grew: for the LORD God had not caused it to rain upon the Earth, and there was not a man to till the ground.

[6] But there went up a mist from the Earth, and watered the whole face of the ground.

[7] And the LORD God formed man of the dust of the ground, and breathed into his nostrils the breath of life; and man became a living soul.

[78] John 14:10

[10] Believest thou not that I am in the Father, and the Father in me? the words that I speak unto you I speak not of myself: but the Father that dwelleth in me, he doeth the works.

[79] 1 Corinthians 13:9-12

[9] For we know in part, and we prophesy in part.

[10] But when that which is perfect is come, then that which is in part shall be done away.

[11] When I was a child, I spake as a child, I understood as a child, I thought as a child: but when I became a man, I put away childish things.

[12] For now we see through a glass, darkly; but then face to face: now I know in part; but then shall I know even as also I am known.

[80] Genesis 2: 16,17 & Genesis 3:2,3

[16] And the LORD God commanded the man, saying, Of every tree of the garden thou mayest freely eat:

[17] But of the tree of the knowledge of good and evil, thou shalt not eat of it: for in the day that thou eatest thereof thou shalt surely die.

[2] And the woman said unto the serpent, We may eat of the fruit of the trees of the garden:

[3] But of the fruit of the tree which is in the midst of the garden, God hath said, Ye shall not eat of it, neither shall ye touch it, lest ye die.

[81] Ezekiel 28:2-9, 13-19

(Below in verses 2-9, the separate, alien ego states, "I am a God," and seems to prosper for a time until its inevitable death arrives where the error is revealed, "Wilt thou yet say before him that slayeth thee, I am God? but thou shalt be a man, and no God, in the hand of him that slayeth thee." In verses 13-19 below we find, "Thou hast been in Eden the garden of God; Thou wast perfect in thy ways from the day that thou wast created, till iniquity was found in thee" which of course, is the mistaken belief of being a separate, thinking, creating mind and un-beknownst ego that inadvertently is making the claim, "I am a God." This false ego is destined to perish as do all unreal illusions, "never shalt thou be any more.")

[2] Son of man, say unto the prince of Tyrus, Thus saith the Lord GOD; Because thine heart is lifted up, and thou hast said, I am a God, I sit in the seat of God, in the midst of the seas; yet thou art a man, and not God, though thou set thine heart as the heart of God:

[3] Behold, thou art wiser than Daniel; there is no secret that they can hide from thee:

[4] With thy wisdom and with thine understanding thou hast gotten thee riches, and hast gotten gold and silver into thy treasures:

[5] By thy great wisdom and by thy traffick hast thou increased thy riches, and thine heart is lifted up because of thy riches:

[6] Therefore thus saith the Lord GOD; Because thou hast set thine heart as the heart of God;

[7] Behold, therefore I will bring strangers upon thee, the terrible of the nations: and they shall draw their swords against the beauty of thy wisdom, and they shall defile thy brightness.

[8] They shall bring thee down to the pit, and thou shalt die the deaths of them that are slain in the midst of the seas.

[**9**] Wilt thou yet say before him that slayeth thee, I am God? but thou shalt be a man, and no God, in the hand of him that slayeth thee.

[**13**] Thou hast been in Eden the garden of God; every precious stone was thy covering, the sardius, topaz, and the diamond, the beryl, the onyx, and the jasper, the sapphire, the emerald, and the carbuncle, and gold: the workmanship of thy tabrets and of thy pipes was prepared in thee in the day that thou wast created.
[**14**] Thou art the anointed cherub that covereth; and I have set thee so: thou wast upon the holy mountain of God; thou hast walked up and down in the midst of the stones of fire.
[**15**] Thou wast perfect in thy ways from the day that thou wast created, till iniquity was found in thee.
[**16**] By the multitude of thy merchandise they have filled the midst of thee with violence, and thou hast sinned: therefore I will cast thee as profane out of the mountain of God: and I will destroy thee, O covering cherub, from the midst of the stones of fire.
[**17**] Thine heart was lifted up because of thy beauty, thou hast corrupted thy wisdom by reason of thy brightness: I will cast thee to the ground, I will lay thee before kings, that they may behold thee.
[**18**] Thou hast defiled thy sanctuaries by the multitude of thine iniquities, by the iniquity of thy traffick; therefore will I bring forth a fire from the midst of thee, it shall devour thee, and I will bring thee to ashes upon the Earth in the sight of all them that behold thee.
[**19**] All they that know thee among the people shall be astonished at thee: thou shalt be a terror, and never shalt thou be any more.

[82] John 1:3
[**3**] All things were made by him; and without him was not any thing made that was made.

[83] Revelation 1:8
[**8**] I am Alpha and Omega, the beginning and the ending, saith the Lord, which is, and which was, and which is to come, the Almighty.

[84] Genesis 1:26,27; 2:1; 2:7
(Due to the infinite individuality of the one Life, Intelligence, the "maker" of man in this passage, is referred to in the plural as "us." An analogy here would be the infinite number of rays all manifesting the entire identity of the sun. Of course, the image and likeness of infinite Intelligence could never be the image and likeness of the alien ego, i.e.,

numerous, finite, physical human beings with their separate, multiple egos. There can be only the one, infinite manifestation and awareness of Intelligence itself, the infinite and sole Individual.)

[26] And God said, Let us make man in our image, after our likeness: and let them have dominion over the fish of the sea, and over the fowl of the air, and over the cattle, and over all the Earth, and over every creeping thing that creepeth upon the Earth.
[27] So God created man in his own image, in the image of God created he him; male and female created he them.
(All the ideas of infinite Intelligence are completed and this universe of ideas is Man, the awareness of Self, the only <u>man</u>ifestation or effect of the one cause, Mind.)

[1] Thus the heavens and the Earth were finished, and all the host of them.

(The next passage reveals how the finite, physical human being formed of dust or matter, comes into being, not through the action of God, or the one, infinite, Intelligence as above, but through the action of the LORD God that is actually the alien ego that is referred to as demiurge, yaldabaoth, satan, devil, or the prince of darkness in various ancient texts. It is noted that this takes place <u>after </u>the mist or mystification arose. The words "...and man became a living soul" clearly define the error of believing Life and a thinking Intelligence to reside in and be dependent on a finite shadow-man that is the subjective but unreal manifestation of a mistaken, imagined and alien so-called thinker.)

[7] And the LORD God formed man of the dust of the ground, and breathed into his nostrils the breath of life; and man became a living soul.

[85] Luke 6:43,44
[43] For a good tree bringeth not forth corrupt fruit; neither doth a corrupt tree bring forth good fruit.
[44] For every tree is known by his own fruit. For of thorns men do not gather figs, nor of a bramble bush gather they grapes.

86 Revelation 12:9

[**9**] And the great dragon was cast out, that old serpent, called the Devil, and Satan, which deceiveth the whole world: he was cast out into the Earth, and his angels were cast out with him.

87 Revelation 13:1,2

(The automatic, derivative consequences of believing or claiming to be a separate, alien ego results in the belief of being a separate, finite, material organism, the "beast" below. Therefore, "the dragon" (alien ego), "gave him" (so-called separate, finite, material organism), "his power, and his seat, and great authority" (automatic, derivative results or failures due to the so-called harsh "laws" and "facts" of the illusion of organic life in a material universe).

[**1**] And I stood upon the sand of the sea, and saw a beast rise up out of the sea, having seven heads and ten horns, and upon his horns ten crowns, and upon his heads the name of blasphemy.

[**2**] And the beast which I saw was like unto a leopard, and his feet were as the feet of a bear, and his mouth as the mouth of a lion: and the dragon gave him his power, and his seat, and great authority.

88 John 8:32

[**32**] And ye shall know the truth, and the truth shall make you free.

89 Revelation 13:4,7,8

(The gauntlet is thrown down; who can challenge the validity of the so-called "laws" and "facts" that all must obey in an objective, material universe and overcome them?)

[**4**] And they worshipped the dragon which gave power unto the beast: and they worshipped the beast, saying, Who is like unto the beast? Who is able to make war with him?

[**7**] And it was given unto him to make war with the saints, and to overcome them: and power was given him over all kindreds, and tongues, and nations.

[**8**] And all that dwell upon the Earth shall worship him, whose names are not written in the book of life of the Lamb slain from the foundation of the world.

⁹⁰ 1 John 3:1-3

[1] Behold, what manner of love the Father hath bestowed upon us, that we should be called the sons of God: therefore the world knoweth us not, because it knew him not.

[2] Beloved, now are we the sons of God, and it doth not yet appear what we shall be: but we know that, when he shall appear, we shall be like him; for we shall see him as he is.

[3] And every man that hath this hope in him purifieth himself, even as he is pure.

⁹¹ 2 Thessalonians 2:4

[4] Who opposeth and exalted himself above all that is called God, or that is worshipped; so that he as God sitteth in the temple of God, shewing himself that he is God.

⁹² 2 Thessalonians 2:11

[11] And for this cause God shall send them strong delusion that they should believe a lie:

⁹³ Jeremiah 17:5

[5] Thus saith the LORD; Cursed be the man that trusteth in man, and maketh flesh his arm, and whose heart departeth from the LORD.

⁹⁴ Genesis 3:14-24, Luke 15:11-32

[14] And the LORD God said unto the serpent, Because thou hast done this, thou art cursed above all cattle, and above every beast of the field; upon thy belly shalt thou go, and dust shalt thou eat all the days of thy life:

[15] And I will put enmity between thee and the woman, and between thy seed and her seed; it shall bruise thy head, and thou shalt bruise his heel.

[16] Unto the woman he said, I will greatly multiply thy sorrow and thy conception; in sorrow thou shalt bring forth children; and thy desire shall be to thy husband, and he shall rule over thee.

[17] And unto Adam he said, Because thou hast hearkened unto the voice of thy wife, and hast eaten of the tree, of which I commanded thee, saying, Thou shalt not eat of it: cursed is the ground for thy sake; in sorrow shalt thou eat of it all the days of thy life;

[18] Thorns also and thistles shall it bring forth to thee; and thou shalt eat the herb of the field;

[19] In the sweat of thy face shalt thou eat bread, till thou return unto the ground; for out of it wast thou taken: for dust thou art, and unto dust shalt thou return.

[20] And Adam called his wife's name Eve; because she was the mother of all living.

[21] Unto Adam also and to his wife did the LORD God make coats of skins, and clothed them.

[22] And the LORD God said, Behold, the man is become as one of us, to know good and evil: and now, lest he put forth his hand, and take also of the tree of life, and eat, and live for ever:

[23] Therefore the LORD God sent him forth from the garden of Eden, to till the ground from whence he was taken.

[24] So he drove out the man; and he placed at the east of the garden of Eden Cherubims, and a flaming sword which turned every way, to keep the way of the tree of life.

[11] And he said, A certain man had two sons:

[12] And the younger of them said to his father, Father, give me the portion of goods that falleth to me. And he divided unto them his living.

[13] And not many days after the younger son gathered all together, and took his journey into a far country, and there wasted his substance with riotous living.

[14] And when he had spent all, there arose a mighty famine in that land; and he began to be in want.

[15] And he went and joined himself to a citizen of that country; and he sent him into his fields to feed swine.

[16] And he would fain have filled his belly with the husks that the swine did eat: and no man gave unto him.

[17] And when he came to himself, he said, How many hired servants of my father's have bread enough and to spare, and I perish with hunger!

[18] I will arise and go to my father, and will say unto him, Father, I have sinned against heaven, and before thee,

[19] And am no more worthy to be called thy son: make me as one of thy hired servants.

[20] And he arose, and came to his father. But when he was yet a great way off, his father saw him, and had compassion, and ran, and fell on his neck, and kissed him.

[**21**] And the son said unto him, Father, I have sinned against heaven, and in thy sight, and am no more worthy to be called thy son.

[**22**] But the father said to his servants, Bring forth the best robe, and put it on him; and put a ring on his hand, and shoes on his feet:

[**23**] And bring hither the fatted calf, and kill it; and let us eat, and be merry:

[**24**] For this my son was dead, and is alive again; he was lost, and is found. And they began to be merry.

[**25**] Now his elder son was in the field: and as he came and drew nigh to the house, he heard music and dancing.

[**26**] And he called one of the servants, and asked what these things meant.

[**27**] And he said unto him, Thy brother is come; and thy father hath killed the fatted calf, because he hath received him safe and sound.

[**28**] And he was angry, and would not go in: therefore came his father out, and intreated him.

[**29**] And he answering said to his father, Lo, these many years do I serve thee, neither transgressed I at any time thy commandment: and yet thou never gavest me a kid, that I might make merry with my friends:

[**30**] But as soon as this thy son was come, which hath devoured thy living with harlots, thou hast killed for him the fatted calf.

[**31**] And he said unto him, Son, thou art ever with me, and all that I have is thine.

[**32**] It was meet that we should make merry, and be glad: for this thy brother was dead, and is alive again; and was lost, and is found.

[95] Habakkuk 1:13

[**13**] Thou art of purer eyes than to behold evil, and canst not look on iniquity:

[96] *The Gnostic Bible,* in "The Gospel of Philip," excerpts below from paragraphs entitled, "Laughing Christ" and "Creation," page 286:

> As soon as Christ went down into the water
> He came out laughing at everything in this world,
> Not because he thought it a trifle, but out of contempt.
> Whoever wants to enter the kingdom of heaven will do so.
> Whoever despises everything in this world, scorns it as a trifle,
> Will emerge laughing.

The world came into being through error.
The agent who made it
Wanted it to be imperishable and immortal.
He failed. He came up with less than his desire.
The world was never incorruptible,
Nor was its maker.

[97] Revelation 17:1-8
(All false, erroneous ideas of a separate, alien ego are simply illusions as in the metaphor, "…they behold the beast that was, and is not, and yet is." Believing in life or mind to be separated from the only Life and Mind will result in the worthless, counterfeit birth-life-death experience, "and they that dwell on the Earth shall wonder, whose names were not written in the book of life from the foundation of the world, when they behold the beast that was, and is not, and yet is.")
[1] And there came one of the seven angels which had the seven vials, and talked with me, saying unto me, Come hither; I will shew unto thee the judgment of the great whore that sitteth upon many waters:
[2] With whom the kings of the Earth have committed fornication, and the inhabitants of the Earth have been made drunk with the wine of her fornication.
[3] So he carried me away in the spirit into the wilderness: and I saw a woman sit upon a scarlet coloured beast, full of names of blasphemy, having seven heads and ten horns.
[4] And the woman was arrayed in purple and scarlet colour, and decked with gold and precious stones and pearls, having a golden cup in her hand full of abominations and filthiness of her fornication:
[5] And upon her forehead was a name written, MYSTERY, BABYLON THE GREAT, THE MOTHER OF HARLOTS AND ABOMINATIONS OF THE EARTH.
[6] And I saw the woman drunken with the blood of the saints, and with the blood of the martyrs of Jesus: and when I saw her, I wondered with great admiration.
[7] And the angel said unto me, Wherefore didst thou marvel? I will tell thee the mystery of the woman, and of the beast that carrieth her, which hath the seven heads and ten horns.
[8] The beast that thou sawest was, and is not; and shall ascend out of the bottomless pit, and go into perdition: and they that dwell on the Earth shall wonder, whose names were not written in the book of life from the foundation of the world, when they behold the beast that was, and is not, and yet is.

[98] John 6:35, Matthew 4:1-4

(The Truth that Jesus is laboring to explain is the true, food of Life. Here, the phrase, "...he that cometh to me..." and "...he that believeth on me..." is taken to mean he that seeks out and <u>understands</u> the Truth, that are his teachings and are the true, food of Life.)

[35] And Jesus said unto them, I am the bread of life: he that cometh to me shall never hunger; and he that believeth on me shall never thirst.

[1] Then was Jesus led up of the Spirit into the wilderness to be tempted of the devil.

[2] And when he had fasted forty days and forty nights, he was afterward an hungred.

[3] And when the tempter came to him, he said, If thou be the Son of God, command that these stones be made bread.

[4] But he answered and said, It is written, Man shall not live by bread alone, but by every word that proceedeth out of the mouth of God.

[99] John 8:32

[32] And ye shall know the truth, and the truth shall make you free.

[100] Job 3:3-5, Luke 23:27-29

[3] Let the day perish wherein I was born, and the night in which it was said, There is a man child conceived.

[4] Let that day be darkness; let not God regard it from above, neither let the light shine upon it.

[5] Let darkness and the shadow of death stain it; let a cloud dwell upon it; let the blackness of the day terrify it.

[27] And there followed him a great company of people, and of women, which also bewailed and lamented him.

[28] But Jesus turning unto them said, Daughters of Jerusalem, weep not for me, but weep for yourselves, and for your children.

[29] For, behold, the days are coming, in the which they shall say, Blessed are the barren, and the wombs that never bare, and the paps which never gave suck.

[101] John 10:20-38

[20] And many of them said, He hath a devil, and is mad; why hear ye him?

[21] Others said, These are not the words of him that hath a devil. Can a devil open the eyes of the blind?

[22] And it was at Jerusalem the feast of the dedication, and it was winter.

[23] And Jesus walked in the temple in Solomon's porch.

[24] Then came the Jews round about him, and said unto him, How long dost thou make us to doubt? If thou be the Christ, tell us plainly.

[25] Jesus answered them, I told you, and ye believed not: the works that I do in my Father's name, they bear witness of me.

[26] But ye believe not, because ye are not of my sheep, as I said unto you.

[27] My sheep hear my voice, and I know them, and they follow me:

[28] And I give unto them eternal life; and they shall never perish, neither shall any man pluck them out of my hand.

[29] My Father, which gave them me, is greater than all; and no man is able to pluck them out of my Father's hand.

[30] I and my Father are one.

[31] Then the Jews took up stones again to stone him.

[32] Jesus answered them, Many good works have I shewed you from my Father; for which of those works do ye stone me?

[33] The Jews answered him, saying, For a good work we stone thee not; but for blasphemy; and because that thou, being a man, makest thyself God.

[34] Jesus answered them, Is it not written in your law, I said, Ye are gods?

[35] If he called them gods, unto whom the word of God came, and the scripture cannot be broken;

[36] Say ye of him, whom the Father hath sanctified, and sent into the world, Thou blasphemes; because I said, I am the Son of God?

[37] If I do not the works of my Father, believe me not.

[38] But if I do, though ye believe not me, believe the works: that ye may know, and believe, that the Father is in me, and I in him.

[102] John 8:38-45
(Clearly below, Jesus is making the distinction between two different fathers (causes) and their respective offspring (conscious awareness). One, the true Father, the only Intelligence whose reflected effect is its awareness and consciousness of the Truth of perfect oneness. The other, the false father, a murderer and a liar, the separate, alien ego whose highest awareness or effect is the imperfect human being victimized and trapped in a meat-sack body, reproducing and going through its seemingly endless, troublesome and pitiful birth-life-death cycles.)

[38] I speak that which I have seen with my Father: and ye do that which ye have seen with your father.

[39] They answered and said unto him, Abraham is our father. Jesus saith unto them, If ye were Abraham's children, ye would do the works of Abraham.

[40] But now ye seek to kill me, a man that hath told you the truth, which I have heard of God: this did not Abraham.

[41] Ye do the deeds of your father. Then said they to him, We be not born of fornication; we have one Father, even God.

[42] Jesus said unto them, If God were your Father, ye would love me: for I proceeded forth and came from God; neither came I of myself, but he sent me.

[43] Why do ye not understand my speech? even because ye cannot hear my word.

[44] Ye are of your father the devil, and the lusts of your father ye will do. He was a murderer from the beginning, and abode not in the truth, because there is no truth in him. When he speaketh a lie, he speaketh of his own: for he is a liar, and the father of it.

[45] And because I tell you the truth, ye believe me not.

[103] John 5:30,31

[30] I can of mine own self do nothing: as I hear, I judge: and my judgment is just; because I seek not mine own will, but the will of the Father which hath sent me.

[31] If I bear witness of myself, my witness is not true.

[104] John 10:7-10

(Note below, "*I am* the door," and "I am come that they might have life, and that they might have it more abundantly." There is a thief that comes to steal your identity, resulting in death and destruction.)

[7] Then said Jesus unto them again, Verily, verily, I say unto you, I am the door of the sheep.

[8] All that ever came before me are thieves and robbers: but the sheep did not hear them.

[9] I am the door: by me if any man enter in, he shall be saved, and shall go in and out, and find pasture.

[10] The thief cometh not, but for to steal, and to kill, and to destroy: I am come that they might have life, and that they might have it more abundantly.

105 Ephesians 6:12

[12] For we wrestle not against flesh and blood, but against principalities, against powers, against the rulers of the darkness of this world, against spiritual wickedness in high places.

("high places" is, of course, reaching the understanding that your mind, consciousness, is the highest and only "place" in reality.)

106 Matthew 24:15

[15] When ye therefore shall see the abomination of desolation, spoken of by Daniel the prophet, stand in the holy place, (whoso readeth, let him understand:)

(Again, the "holy place" is, of course, your mind, the only "place" and is where we now *see and understand* the abomination - the alien ego!)

107 Romans 3:4 and Revelation 13:18

(In the verses below, the alien human ego, "man" is equated to being a "liar" and a "beast," and there is also a reference to the number "666." The true Universe (Man) that is the image and likeness of Intelligence (God) was manifested in "seven days" in Genesis and is the only reality; complete and perfect. Therefore, in Genesis the number seven signifies perfection and completeness, "and he rested on the seventh day from all his work which he had made."

The number 6, on the other hand, indicates not quite reaching the mark, a falling short as a disingenuous counterfeit, a cheap imitation. Also, the three place number (666) suggests a reference to the three segments or trinity in the structure of creative consciousness; that is, mind (father) with its conscious knowing and feeling (offspring of mind or its son) to manifest any idea, fact or illusion (the whole ghost—its expressed whole universe of ideas). Within reality, within I AM resides all Intelligence with its knowing of the Truth and its ensuing feeling of perfection and love about this Truth and the harmonious facts that are consequently manifested. Truly the Father, the Son, and the Whole and Perfect Ghost or reflected manifestation of Intelligence. Numerically, the three segments of the trinity of the true Mind and its full awareness of its infinite ideas could be represented as "777" because all seven faculties are present and perfect; that of seeing, hearing, touching, tasting, smelling, reasoning, and understanding correctly.

Again, and on the other hand, the creative trinity of the human mind could be represented numerically as "666" because only six mistaken, belief faculties are present; that of limited seeing, hearing,

touching, tasting, smelling, faulty reasoning, and <u>no</u> understanding of the Truth. Only six mistaken belief-senses are present in the creative trinity of the counterfeit, alien, human ego. The seventh, the correct understanding of the Truth is missing rendering the structure of the alien ego deranged; its mind is imagined (the other father Jesus referred to as the liar and murderer), its conscious "knowing" is mistaken and its feelings are inharmonious, vulnerable and fearful (offspring of mind or its son) that all together, manifest inharmonious illusions (a very "unholy" ghost illusion of so-called material beings in a material universe). Hence "666" indicates the counterfeit alien ego, "Let him that hath understanding count the number of the beast: for it is the number of a man;" the blind and lost separated, human ego and its illusions.)
[4] ... let God be true, but every man a liar; ...

[18] Here is wisdom. Let him that hath understanding count the number of the beast: for it is the number of a man; and his number is Six hundred threescore and six.

[108] Luke 23:34
[34] Then said Jesus, Father, forgive them; for they know not what they do. And they parted his raiment, and cast lots.

[109] Romans 7:17-20
[17] Now then it is no more I that do it, but sin that dwelleth in me.
[18] For I know that in me (that is, in my flesh,) dwelleth no good thing: for to will is present with me; but how to perform that which is good I find not.
[19] For the good that I would I do not: but the evil which I would not, that I do.
[20] Now if I do that I would not, it is no more I that do it, but sin that dwelleth in me.

[110] Matthew 6:14,15
[14] For if ye forgive men their trespasses, your heavenly Father will also forgive you:
[15] But if ye forgive not men their trespasses, neither will your Father forgive your trespasses.

[111] Romans 7:22-25
[22] For I delight in the law of God after the inward man:

[**23**] But I see another law in my members, warring against the law of my mind, and bringing me into captivity to the law of sin which is in my members.

[**24**] O wretched man that I am! who shall deliver me from the body of this death?

[**25**] I thank God through Jesus Christ our Lord. So then with the mind I myself serve the law of God; but with the flesh the law of sin.

¹¹² John 8:32

[**32**] And ye shall know the truth, and the truth shall make you free.

¹¹³ Luke 12:29-32

[**29**] And seek not ye what ye shall eat, or what ye shall drink, neither be ye of doubtful mind.

[**30**] For all these things do the nations of the world seek after: and your Father knoweth that ye have need of these things.

[**31**] But rather seek ye the kingdom of God; and all these things shall be added unto you.

[**32**] Fear not, little flock; for it is your Father's good pleasure to give you the kingdom.

¹¹⁴ Job 3:25

(Clearly this verse in the Book of Job is bringing out the necessary element of fear for hypnotic lies to "appear.")

[**25**] For the thing which I greatly feared is come upon me, and that which I was afraid of is come unto me.

¹¹⁵ Matthew 5:25, 26

(The word "Agree" is obviously taken as either "agree to disagree" or a typographical error for the word "disagree" because agreeing with the adversary, the alien ego and its lies and suggestions only results in suffering through the hypnotic lie, "thou be cast into prison...till thou hast paid the uttermost farthing.")

[**25**] Agree with thine adversary quickly, whiles thou art in the way with him; lest at any time the adversary deliver thee to the judge, and the judge deliver thee to the officer, and thou be cast into prison.

[**26**] Verily I say unto thee, Thou shalt by no means come out thence, till thou hast paid the uttermost farthing.

[116] John 10:30

(The only entity that can exist in addition to pure and infinite Intelligence is ITS OWN AWARENESS OF ITS INFINITE SELF as explained in Jesus' metaphor below. One Mind (Father, source of all) and its conscious awareness of itself (its only offspring, the Son). The use of the term Father was not gender related but was used to signify source. Some texts use the term Father-Mother for this source of Being. There are no *separate* male and female elements in true Being for these attributes are One. These *separated* phenomena only exists in the illusion of the separated ego.)

[**30**] I and *my* Father are one.

[117] Romans 8:16-18

[**16**] The Spirit itself beareth witness with our spirit, that we are the children of God:

[**17**] And if children, then heirs; heirs of God, and joint-heirs with Christ; if so be that we suffer with him, that we may be also glorified together.

[**18**] For I reckon that the sufferings of this present time are not worthy to be compared with the glory which shall be revealed in us.

[118] John 8:32

[**32**] And ye shall know the truth, and the truth shall make you free.

[119] John 14:13-18

[**13**] And whatsoever ye shall ask in my name, that will I do, that the Father may be glorified in the Son.

[**14**] If ye shall ask any thing in my name, I will do it.

[**15**] If ye love me, keep my commandments.

[**16**] And I will pray the Father, and he shall give you another Comforter, that he may abide with you for ever;

[**17**] Even the Spirit of truth; whom the world cannot receive, because it seeth him not, neither knoweth him: but ye know him; for he dwelleth with you, and shall be in you.

[**18**] I will not leave you comfortless: I will come to you.

[120] John 8:44

[**44**] Ye are of your father the devil, and the lusts of your father ye will do. He was a murderer from the beginning, and abode not in the truth, because there is no truth in him. When he speaketh a lie, he speaketh of his own: for he is a liar, and the father of it.

121 Matthew 6:31-33

[**31**] Therefore take no thought, saying, What shall we eat? or, What shall we drink? or, Wherewithal shall we be clothed?

[**32**] (For after all these things do the Gentiles seek:) for your heavenly Father knoweth that ye have need of all these things.

[**33**] But seek ye first the kingdom of God, and his righteousness; and all these things shall be added unto you.

122 John 14:12

[**12**] Verily, verily, I say unto you, He that believeth on me, the works that I do shall he do also; and greater works than these shall he do; because I go unto my Father.

123 Genesis 3:9,10

[**9**] And the Lord God called unto Adam, and said unto him, Where *art* thou?

[**10**] And he said, I heard thy voice in the garden and I was afraid, because I *was* naked; and I hid myself.

124 Job 3:25

[**25**] For the thing which I greatly feared is come upon me, and that which I was afraid of is come unto me.

125 Matthew 12:35

[**35**] A good man out of the good treasure of the heart bringeth forth good things: and an evil man out of the evil treasure bringeth forth evil things.

126 Luke 12:31

[**31**] But rather seek ye the kingdom of God; and all these things shall be added unto you.

127 Proverbs 23:7 (excerpt)

[**7**] For as he thinketh in his heart, so is he:

128 Genesis 1:27,28

[**27**] So God created man in his own image, in the image of God created he him; male and female created he them.

[**28**] And God blessed them, and God said unto them, Be fruitful, and multiply, and replenish the Earth, and subdue it: and have dominion

over the fish of the sea, and over the fowl of the air, and over every living thing that moveth upon the Earth.

129 Matthew 10:28
[28] And fear not them which kill the body, but are not able to kill the soul: but rather fear him which is able to destroy both soul and body in hell.

130 John 7:24
[24] Judge not according to the appearance, but judge righteous judgment.

131 1 John 4:18
[18] There is no fear in love; but perfect love casteth out fear: because fear hath torment. He that feareth is not made perfect in love.

132 Matthew 19:17, Genesis 1:31
[17] And he said unto him, Why callest thou me good? there is none good but one, that is, God: but if thou wilt enter into life, keep the commandments.

[31] And God saw every thing that he had made, and, behold, it was very good. And the evening and the morning were the sixth day.

133 Philippians 2:5,6
[5] Let this mind be in you, which was also in Christ Jesus:
[6] Who, being in the form of God, thought it not robbery to be equal with God:

134 Matthew 6:6
[6] But thou, when thou prayest, enter into thy closet, and when thou hast shut thy door, pray to thy Father which is in secret; and thy Father which seeth in secret shall reward thee openly.

135 Colossians 3:1-15
(The only offspring of infinite Mind, of infinite Intelligence is the active understanding and conscious awareness of itself as infinite perfection, good, eternal Life, Truth and Love, all of which are Christ, the "offspring" or "Son" of infinite Intelligence, God, good.)
[1] If ye then be risen with Christ, seek those things which are above, where Christ sitteth on the right hand of God.

[2] Set your affection on things above, not on things on the Earth.

[3] For ye are dead, and your life is hid with Christ in God.

[4] When Christ, who is our life, shall appear, then shall ye also appear with him in glory.

[5] Mortify therefore your members which are upon the Earth; fornication, uncleanness, inordinate affection, evil concupiscence, and covetousness, which is idolatry:

[6] For which things' sake the wrath of God cometh on the children of disobedience:

[7] In the which ye also walked some time, when ye lived in them.

[8] But now ye also put off all these; anger, wrath, malice, blasphemy, filthy communication out of your mouth.

[9] Lie not one to another, seeing that ye have put off the old man with his deeds;

[10] And have put on the new man, which is renewed in knowledge after the image of him that created him:

[11] Where there is neither Greek nor Jew, circumcision nor uncircumcision, Barbarian, Scythian, bond nor free: but Christ is all, and in all.

[12] Put on therefore, as the elect of God, holy and beloved, bowels of mercies, kindness, humbleness of mind, meekness, longsuffering;

[13] Forbearing one another, and forgiving one another, if any man have a quarrel against any: even as Christ forgave you, so also do ye.

[14] And above all these things put on charity, which is the bond of perfectness.

[15] And let the peace of God rule in your hearts, to the which also ye are called in one body; and be ye thankful.

[136] John 8:44

(In addition to the one good and true Father that Jesus constantly associates himself with, Jesus uncovers another "father", the "alien" father that is a liar and the source of all lies.)

[44] Ye are of your father the devil, and the lusts of your father ye will do. He was a murderer from the beginning, and abode not in the truth, because there is no truth in him. When he speaketh a lie, he speaketh of his own: for he is a liar, and the father of it.

[137] Hartmann, W. K., R.J. Phillips, and G.J. Taylor, eds. *Origin of the Moon.* (Houston: Lunar and Planetary Institute, 1986.), 1 John 2:18-19

[18] Little children, it is the last time: and as ye have heard that antichrist shall come, even now are there many antichrists; whereby we know that it is the last time.

[19] They went out from us, but they were not of us; for if they had been of us, they would no doubt have continued with us: but they went out, that they might be made manifest that they were not all of us.

138 Genesis 2:7, 3:22 (excerpt)
(Both passages below observe that "man," that is, ma<u>ni</u>festation, the projected mental idea or effect, the image and likeness up there on the movie screen of awareness, has become the *substance* of life itself - consciousness! What an outrageous and ludicrous mistake it is when we believe consciousness is wholly and mysteriously contained within one of its finite ideas, a brain, that is no-thing more than a projected and mistaken image on the screen! The brain and its attendant body are simply subjective illusion-ideas or shadows with absolutely no substance of their own to do or think anything!! The image and likeness of the separate, ignorant, idiotic, alien ego - a mere image - to now think it has become the substance of mentality, consciousness and life receives the mocking observation from the true facts of Life, "Behold the man is become one of us"! A mere shadow claiming to be the very source of the shadow!) (Behold, the effect, a mere reflection, actually and erroneously believes it has become the cause!)
[7] And the LORD God formed man of the dust of the ground, and breathed into his nostrils the breath of life; and man became a living soul.

[22] And the LORD God said, Behold, the man is become as one of us,

139 Revelation 12
(The woman below "clothed with the sun, and the moon under her feet" is the wakening of Intelligence, Truth and especially Love that has finally understood and overcame the hypnotic dream generated by the imagined alien and separate ego - "the moon under her feet, and upon her head a crown of twelve stars.")
[1] And there appeared a great wonder in heaven; a woman clothed with the sun, and the moon under her feet, and upon her head a crown of twelve stars:
[2] And she being with child cried, travailing in birth, and pained to be delivered.

[3] And there appeared another wonder in heaven; and behold a great red dragon, having seven heads and ten horns, and seven crowns upon his heads.

[4] And his tail drew the third part of the stars of heaven, and did cast them to the Earth: and the dragon stood before the woman which was ready to be delivered, for to devour her child as soon as it was born.

[5] And she brought forth a man child, who was to rule all nations with a rod of iron: and her child was caught up unto God, and to his throne.

[6] And the woman fled into the wilderness, where she hath a place prepared of God, that they should feed her there a thousand two hundred and threescore days.

[7] And there was war in heaven: Michael and his angels fought against the dragon; and the dragon fought and his angels,

[8] And prevailed not; neither was their place found any more in heaven.

[9] And the great dragon was cast out, that old serpent, called the Devil, and Satan, which deceiveth the whole world: he was cast out into the Earth, and his angels were cast out with him.

[10] And I heard a loud voice saying in heaven, Now is come salvation, and strength, and the kingdom of our God, and the power of his Christ: for the accuser of our brethren is cast down, which accused them before our God day and night.

[11] And they overcame him by the blood of the Lamb, and by the word of their testimony; and they loved not their lives unto the death.

[12] Therefore rejoice, ye heavens, and ye that dwell in them. Woe to the inhabiters of the Earth and of the sea! for the devil is come down unto you, having great wrath, because he knoweth that he hath but a short time.

[13] And when the dragon saw that he was cast unto the Earth, he persecuted the woman which brought forth the man child.

[14] And to the woman were given two wings of a great eagle, that she might fly into the wilderness, into her place, where she is nourished for a time, and times, and half a time, from the face of the serpent.

[15] And the serpent cast out of his mouth water as a flood after the woman, that he might cause her to be carried away of the flood.

[16] And the Earth helped the woman, and the Earth opened her mouth, and swallowed up the flood which the dragon cast out of his mouth.

[17] And the dragon was wroth with the woman, and went to make war with the remnant of her seed, which keep the commandments of God, and have the testimony of Jesus Christ.

140 Department of Energy, Energy Citations Database.

141 See ITER.org for information on Fusion Energy Development

142 Matthew 24:29, 35
[29] Immediately after the tribulation of those days shall the sun be darkened, and the moon shall not give her light, and the stars shall fall from heaven, and the powers of the heavens shall be shaken:

[35] Heaven and Earth shall pass away, but my words shall not pass away.

143 Matthew 6:22-24
(In the passage below, taking the interpretation of the "eye" and "body" literally as physical phenomenon renders the meaning of the passage vague and senseless. "Eye" is herein understood to mean "I" or ego from which existence is viewed by the individual and "body" is your re-vealed awareness or manifestation of that ego. In reality there is only one single "I" or point of view and that is one, infinite Intelligence, Soul and Ego that we all find ourselves to be when enlightened from the erroneous, separate human sense. Our body is then the manifesta-tion of our infinite Intelligence and Ego—the Identity of one, celestial Universe in its entirety, full of light.)
[22] The light of the body is the eye: if therefore thine eye be single, thy whole body shall be full of light.
[23] But if thine eye be evil, thy whole body shall be full of darkness. If therefore the light that is in thee be darkness, how great is that dark-ness!
[24] No man can serve two masters: for either he will hate the one, and love the other; or else he will hold to the one, and despise the other. Ye cannot serve God and mammon.

144 Ephesians 6:12
[12] For we wrestle not against flesh and blood, but against principal-ities, against powers, against the rulers of the darkness of this world, against spiritual wickedness in high places.

145 John 1:1-5
[1] In the beginning was the Word, and the Word was with God, and the Word was God.
[2] The same was in the beginning with God.

[3] All things were made by him; and without him was not any thing made that was made.

[4] In him was life; and the life was the light of men.

[5] And the light shineth in darkness; and the darkness comprehended it not.

146 Genesis 1:26 (excerpt)

[26] And God said, Let us make man in our image, after our likeness:

147 John 10:30, Luke 6:43-45

[30] I and *my* Father are one.

[43] For a good tree bringeth not forth corrupt fruit; neither doth a corrupt tree bring forth good fruit.

[44] For every tree is known by his own fruit. For of thorns men do not gather figs, nor of a bramble bush gather they grapes.

[45] A good man out of the good treasure of his heart bringeth forth that which is good; and an evil man out of the evil treasure of his heart bringeth forth that which is evil: for of the abundance of the heart his mouth speaketh.

148 John 17:20-24

(These verses stress the perfect oneness of being that has always existed even before the illusion of a material world or a physical Big Bang universe was inadvertently conceived ("before the foundation of the world."))

[20] Neither pray I for these alone, but for them also which shall believe on me through their word;

[21] That they all may be one; as thou, Father, art in me, and I in thee, that they also may be one in us: that the world may believe that thou hast sent me.

[22] And the glory which thou gavest me I have given them; that they may be one, even as we are one:

[23] I in them, and thou in me, that they may be made perfect in one; and that the world may know that thou hast sent me, and hast loved them, as thou hast loved me.

[24] Father, I will that they also, whom thou hast given me, be with me where I am; that they may behold my glory, which thou hast given me: for thou lovedst me before the foundation of the world.

[149] *The Gnostic Bible,* Islamic Literature, *The Mother of Books*, paragraph entitled, "Humans Are Evicted from Paradise," excerpt, page 718: "When the high king came in, he howled against the lingerers, "Get out of here, all of you. Get out of paradise. Assume the form of thin dark shadows." He hurled them away into their shadowy shape, and had women appear with deep vaginas and with breasts."

[150] *The Gnostic Bible,* in "The Gospel of Philip," paragraph entitled, "Seeing," page 270:

> SEEING
> It is impossible to see anything in the real realm
> Unless you become it.
> Not so in the world. You see the sun without being the sun,
> See sky and Earth but are not them.
> This is the truth of the world.
> In the other truth you are what you see.
> If you see spirit, you are spirit.
> If you look at the anointed, you are the anointed.
> If you see the father, you will be the father.
> In this world you see everything but yourself,
> But there, you look at yourself and are what you see.

[151] Matthew 24:14
("…and then shall the end come" below, is, of course, the termination of the big bang illusion and its imagined cause when the good-spell of the one, perfect, and eternal Being is understood.)
[14] And this gospel of the kingdom shall be preached in all the world for a witness unto all nations; and then shall the end come.

[152] Matthew 24:37-41
[37] But as the days of Noe were, so shall also the coming of the Son of man be.
[38] For as in the days that were before the flood they were eating and drinking, marrying and giving in marriage, until the day that Noe entered into the ark,
[39] And knew not until the flood came, and took them all away; so shall also the coming of the Son of man be.
[40] Then shall two be in the field; the one shall be taken, and the other left.
[41] Two women shall be grinding at the mill; the one shall be taken, and the other left.

153 Matthew 7:7,8

[7] Ask, and it shall be given you; seek, and ye shall find; knock, and it shall be opened unto you:

[8] For every one that asketh receiveth; and he that seeketh findeth; and to him that knocketh it shall be opened.

154 Matthew 10:7-14

(Simply dismiss from your thoughts, as you would shake the dust off your shoes, the illusion of those who reject this understanding. This may be done quite casually because the whole rejection-episode is just more inharmonious, hypnotic illusions foisted up by that imagined, separate, alien ego.)

[7] And as ye go, preach, saying, The kingdom of heaven is at hand.

[8] Heal the sick, cleanse the lepers, raise the dead, cast out devils: freely ye have received, freely give.

[9] Provide neither gold, nor silver, nor brass in your purses,

[10] Nor scrip for your journey, neither two coats, neither shoes, nor yet staves: for the workman is worthy of his meat.

[11] And into whatsoever city or town ye shall enter, inquire who in it is worthy; and there abide till ye go thence.

[12] And when ye come into an house, salute it.

[13] And if the house be worthy, let your peace come upon it: but if it be not worthy, let your peace return to you.

[14] And whosoever shall not receive you, nor hear your words, when ye depart out of that house or city, shake off the dust of your feet.

155 Matthew 7:6

[6] Give not that which is holy unto the dogs, neither cast ye your pearls before swine, lest they trample them under their feet, and turn again and rend you.

156 Matthew 10:32-36

[32] Whosoever therefore shall confess me before men, him will I confess also before my Father which is in heaven.

[33] But whosoever shall deny me before men, him will I also deny before my Father which is in heaven.

[34] Think not that I am come to send peace on Earth: I came not to send peace, but a sword.

[35] For I am come to set a man at variance against his father, and the daughter against her mother, and the daughter in law against her mother in law.

[36] And a man's foes shall be they of his own household.

157 Mark 4:3-20

[3] Hearken; Behold, there went out a sower to sow:

[4] And it came to pass, as he sowed, some fell by the way side, and the fowls of the air came and devoured it up.

[5] And some fell on stony ground, where it had not much Earth; and immediately it sprang up, because it had no depth of Earth:

[6] But when the sun was up, it was scorched; and because it had no root, it withered away.

[7] And some fell among thorns, and the thorns grew up, and choked it, and it yielded no fruit.

[8] And other fell on good ground, and did yield fruit that sprang up and increased; and brought forth, some thirty, and some sixty, and some an hundred.

[9] And he said unto them, He that hath ears to hear, let him hear.

[10] And when he was alone, they that were about him with the twelve asked of him the parable.

[11] And he said unto them, Unto you it is given to know the mystery of the kingdom of God: but unto them that are without, all these things are done in parables:

[12] That seeing they may see, and not perceive; and hearing they may hear, and not understand; lest at any time they should be converted, and their sins should be forgiven them.

[13] And he said unto them, Know ye not this parable? and how then will ye know all parables?

[14] The sower soweth the word.

[15] And these are they by the way side, where the word is sown; but when they have heard, Satan cometh immediately, and taketh away the word that was sown in their hearts.

[16] And these are they likewise which are sown on stony ground; who, when they have heard the word, immediately receive it with gladness;

[17] And have no root in themselves, and so endure but for a time: afterward, when affliction or persecution ariseth for the word's sake, immediately they are offended.

[18] And these are they which are sown among thorns; such as hear the word,

[19] And the cares of this world, and the deceitfulness of riches, and the lusts of other things entering in, choke the word, and it becometh unfruitful.

[20] And these are they which are sown on good ground; such as hear the word, and receive it, and bring forth fruit, some thirtyfold, some sixty, and some an hundred.

[158] John 14:16,17

[16] And I will pray the Father, and he shall give you another Comforter, that he may abide with you for ever;

[17] Even the Spirit of truth; whom the world cannot receive, because it seeth him not, neither knoweth him: but ye know him; for he dwelleth with you, and shall be in you.

[159] John 14:12-14

(In the verses below, "I" of course, is the *only* I in existence and is Intelligence, the Father. Its Offspring, the Son, is Individual understanding, conviction and awareness of its own Oneness and Perfection everywhere.)

[12] Verily, verily, I say unto you, He that believeth on me, the works that I do shall he do also; and greater works than these shall he do; because I go unto my Father.

[13] And whatsoever ye shall ask in my name, that will I do, that the Father may be glorified in the Son.

[14] If ye shall ask any thing in my name, I will do it.

[160] John 9:1-5

(Jesus knows his *own* mind and universe caused this incident and illusion to appear—and disappear!)

[1] And as Jesus passed by, he saw a man which was blind from his birth.

[2] And his disciples asked him, saying, Master, who did sin, this man, or his parents, that he was born blind?

[3] Jesus answered, Neither hath this man sinned, nor his parents: but that the works of God should be made manifest in him.

[4] I must work the works of him that sent me, while it is day: the night cometh, when no man can work.

[5] As long as I am in the world, I am the light of the world.

[161] Matthew 23:25-28

25] Woe unto you, scribes and Pharisees, hypocrites! for ye make clean the outside of the cup and of the platter, but within they are full of extortion and excess.

[26] Thou blind Pharisee, cleanse first that which is within the cup and platter, that the outside of them may be clean also.

[27] Woe unto you, scribes and Pharisees, hypocrites! for ye are like unto whited sepulchres, which indeed appear beautiful outward, but are within full of dead men's bones, and of all uncleanness.

[28] Even so ye also outwardly appear righteous unto men, but within ye are full of hypocrisy and iniquity.

162 Matthew 24:48-51

[48] But and if that evil servant shall say in his heart, My lord delayeth his coming;

[49] And shall begin to smite his fellowservants, and to eat and drink with the drunken;

[50] The lord of that servant shall come in a day when he looketh not for him, and in an hour that he is not aware of,

[51] And shall cut him asunder, and appoint him his portion with the hypocrites: there shall be weeping and gnashing of teeth.

163 Mark 9:43-48

[43] And if thy hand offend thee, cut it off: it is better for thee to enter into life maimed, than having two hands to go into hell, into the fire that never shall be quenched:

[44] Where their worm dieth not, and the fire is not quenched.

[45] And if thy foot offend thee, cut it off: it is better for thee to enter halt into life, than having two feet to be cast into hell, into the fire that never shall be quenched:

[46] Where their worm dieth not, and the fire is not quenched.

[47] And if thine eye offend thee, pluck it out: it is better for thee to enter into the kingdom of God with one eye, than having two eyes to be cast into hell fire:

[48] Where their worm dieth not, and the fire is not quenched.

164 Luke 12:4, 5

[4] And I say unto you my friends, Be not afraid of them that kill the body, and after that have no more that they can do.

[5] But I will forewarn you whom ye shall fear: Fear him, which after he hath killed hath power to cast into hell; yea, I say unto you, Fear him.

165 Luke 21: 25-28

(Truly the "powers of heaven shall be shaken" when it is revealed that the big bang universe is an illusion, a counterfeit fake. As this may be hard to understand at first until the clouds of mystification and confusion abates, the Truth will appear as the "Son of man coming in a cloud....")

[25] And there shall be signs in the sun, and in the moon, and in the stars; and upon the Earth distress of nations, with perplexity; the sea and the waves roaring;

[26] Men's hearts failing them for fear, and for looking after those things which are coming on the Earth: for the powers of heaven shall be shaken.

[27] And then shall they see the Son of man coming in a cloud with power and great glory.

[28] And when these things begin to come to pass, then look up, and lift up your heads; for your redemption draweth nigh.

166 Genesis 3:17

(This passage illustrates the positive nature of failures to uncover and identify an existing error. "...cursed is the ground for thy sake...." The ground of course, is the erring belief of a separate, alien ego manifested as a material, human being and its material universe and environment.)

[17] And unto Adam he said, Because thou hast hearkened unto the voice of thy wife, and hast eaten of the tree, of which I commanded thee, saying, Thou shalt not eat of it: cursed is the ground for thy sake; in sorrow shalt thou eat of it all the days of thy life;

167 Revelation 22:13, John 17:20-24

[13] I am Alpha and Omega, the beginning and the end, the first and the last.

[20] Neither pray I for these alone, but for them also which shall believe on me through their word;

[21] That they all may be one; as thou, Father, art in me, and I in thee, that they also may be one in us: that the world may believe that thou hast sent me.

[22] And the glory which thou gavest me I have given them; that they may be one, even as we are one:

[23] I in them, and thou in me, that they may be made perfect in one; and that the world may know that thou hast sent me, and hast loved them, as thou hast loved me.

[**24**] Father, I will that they also, whom thou hast given me, be with me where I am; that they may behold my glory, which thou hast given me: for thou lovedst me before the foundation of the world.

168 John 15:27
[**27**] And ye also shall bear witness, because ye have been with me from the beginning.

169 Mark 13:31
[**31**] Heaven and Earth shall pass away: but my words shall not pass away.

170 Colossians 3:10, 11
(Erroneous humans and their beliefs about the Truth vanish when the Truth is known and the real man, "after the image of him that created him," Christ reemerges and, "is all, and in all.")
[**10**] And have put on the new man, which is renewed in knowledge after the image of him that created him:
[**11**] Where there is neither Greek nor Jew, circumcision nor uncircumcision, Barbarian, Scythian, bond nor free: but Christ is all, and in all.

171 John 20:23
(The following verse appears after Jesus rose from the human death experience but prior to ascending completely to the infinite Identity of Oneness.)
[**23**] Whose soever sins ye remit, they are remitted unto them; and whose soever sins ye retain, they are retained.

172 Revelation 21:1-7
[**1**] And I saw a new heaven and a new Earth: for the first heaven and the first Earth were passed away; and there was no more sea.
[**2**] And I John saw the holy city, new Jerusalem, coming down from God out of heaven, prepared as a bride adorned for her husband.
[**3**] And I heard a great voice out of heaven saying, Behold, the tabernacle of God is with men, and he will dwell with them, and they shall be his people, and God himself shall be with them, and be their God.
[**4**] And God shall wipe away all tears from their eyes; and there shall be no more death, neither sorrow, nor crying, neither shall there be any more pain: for the former things are passed away.

[5] And he that sat upon the throne said, Behold, I make all things new. And he said unto me, Write: for these words are true and faithful. [6] And he said unto me, It is done. I am Alpha and Omega, the beginning and the end. I will give unto him that is athirst of the fountain of the water of life freely.

[7] He that overcometh shall inherit all things; and I will be his God, and he shall be my son.

[173] John 8:51-59

[51] Verily, verily, I say unto you, If a man keep my saying, he shall never see death.

[52] Then said the Jews unto him, Now we know that thou hast a devil. Abraham is dead, and the prophets; and thou sayest, If a man keep my saying, he shall never taste of death.

[53] Art thou greater than our father Abraham, which is dead? and the prophets are dead: whom makest thou thyself?

[54] Jesus answered, If I honour myself, my honour is nothing: it is my Father that honoureth me; of whom ye say, that he is your God:

[55] Yet ye have not known him; but I know him: and if I should say, I know him not, I shall be a liar like unto you: but I know him, and keep his saying.

[56] Your father Abraham rejoiced to see my day: and he saw it, and was glad.

[57] Then said the Jews unto him, Thou art not yet fifty years old, and hast thou seen Abraham?

[58] Jesus said unto them, Verily, verily, I say unto you, Before Abraham was, I am.

[59] Then took they up stones to cast at him: but Jesus hid himself, and went out of the temple, going through the midst of them, and so passed by.

[174] Matthew 6:22,23

(Again in the passage below, taking the interpretation of the "eye" and "body" literally as physical phenomenon renders the meaning of the passage vague and senseless. "Eye" is understood to mean "I", mind, ego and cause from which existence is *viewed* by the individual and "body" is your awareness, effect, reflection, or manifestation of that "I", mind, ego and cause. In reality there is only one single "I" *point of view* or cause and that is one, infinite Intelligence, Mind and Ego that we all find our true Self to be when enlightened from the erroneous, separate, whacked-out human sense, "...if thine eye be evil." Our body is then the effect, reflection, manifestation and awareness of our infinite

Intelligence and Ego - the Identity of one, celestial and perfectly harmonious Universe in its entirety, "…if therefore thine eye be single, thy whole body shall be full of light.")

[22] The light of the body is the eye: if therefore thine eye be single, thy whole body shall be full of light.

[23] But if thine eye be evil, thy whole body shall be full of darkness. If therefore the light that is in thee be darkness, how great is that darkness!

[175] Revelation 19:6,9-11,15,19, and 20

(Truth, Christ, the voice below proclaims to be identical to us, "thy fellow servant." "Blessed are they" who understand the truth "the marriage supper." Cast out religious deceptions based on blind faith and baseless beliefs in so-called supernatural miracles "the false prophet that wrought miracles" along with a finite, material universe and the human meat-sack illusion "his image" of a separate alien ego "the beast" out of your thoughts as you would any malicious and ignorant lie. With your understanding of the Truth "a sharp sword," all illusions can be terminated "smite the nations" and all so-called supernatural miracles become very natural demonstrations that YOU can reveal in your LIFE right NOW "rule them with a rod of iron!")

[6] And I heard as it were the voice of a great multitude, and as the voice of many waters, and as the voice of mighty thunderings, saying, Alleluia: for the Lord God omnipotent reigneth.

[9] And he saith unto me, Write, Blessed are they which are called unto the marriage supper of the Lamb. And he saith unto me, These are the true sayings of God.

[10] And I fell at his feet to worship him. And he said unto me, See thou do it not: I am thy fellow servant, and of thy brethren that have the testimony of Jesus: worship God: for the testimony of Jesus is the spirit of prophecy.

[11] And I saw heaven opened, and behold a white horse; and he that sat upon him was called Faithful and True, and in righteousness he doth judge and make war.

[15] And out of his mouth goeth a sharp sword, that with it he should smite the nations: and he shall rule them with a rod of iron: and he treadeth the winepress of the fierceness and wrath of Almighty God.

[19] And I saw the beast, and the kings of the Earth, and their armies, gathered together to make war against him that sat on the horse, and against his army

[20] And the beast was taken, and with him the false prophet that wrought miracles before him, with which he deceived them that had received the mark of the beast, and them that worshipped his image. These both were cast alive into a lake of fire burning with brimstone.

[176] Luke 13:23-28

[23] Then said one unto him, Lord, are there few that be saved? And he said unto them,
[24] Strive to enter in at the strait gate: for many, I say unto you, will seek to enter in, and shall not be able.
[25] When once the master of the house is risen up, and hath shut to the door, and ye begin to stand without, and to knock at the door, saying, Lord, Lord, open unto us; and he shall answer and say unto you, I know you not whence ye are:
[26] Then shall ye begin to say, We have eaten and drunk in thy presence, and thou hast taught in our streets.
[27] But he shall say, I tell you, I know you not whence ye are: depart from me, all ye workers of iniquity.
[28] There shall be weeping and gnashing of teeth, when ye shall see Abraham, and Isaac, and Jacob, and all the prophets in the kingdom of God, and you yourselves thrust out.

[177] 1 Corinthians 13:9-11

[9] For we know in part, and we prophesy in part.
[10] But when that which is perfect is come, then that which is in part shall be done away.
[11] When I was a child, I spake as a child, I understood as a child, I thought as a child: but when I became a man, I put away childish things.